# Follow The Ac

## A Very Unofficial Guide to the South West Coast Path

By

John Haughton

ISBN: 978-0-244-92845-2

PublishNation
www.publishnation.co.uk

# INTRODUCTION – A SHORT PRE RAMBLE PREAMBLE

Hello, my name is John and this is a book I've written about walking the 630 miles of the English South West Coast Path. It also includes some photographs I took on this wonderful journey. This is my story of a period of 8 weeks, when at least for a short length of time at the age of nearly 59, I became a totally different person and lived a totally different lifestyle. I experienced and did things that were unique to me and I absolutely loved it. I woke up every morning looking forward to a day that would be almost completely different to any other I had known. All my cares and woes were beaches, coves, bays, valleys, rivers, fields, over the hills and far away. I was floating in a bubble of walking, picture taking and writing about the most spectacular, mesmerising and beguiling scenery to be found anywhere in the world. I was an addict high on the freedom of the outdoor life and usually high up a cliff or a hill somewhere.

First of all though I have to get some confessions out of the way; I'm not a writer, I'd never done any long distance walking previously and I'm definitely not a photographer. Oh and by the way I'm actually from the South East. Significantly though perhaps, my early years were spent very close to the coast and walking on and near beaches. The major inspiration for writing this book came from the members of a SWCP Facebook group. I would write a daily post after each day's walk and also post pictures I'd taken that day. The response I had to these posts was initially extremely unexpected and encouraging and latterly extremely moving and humbling.

Ok, so for the uninitiated what exactly is the South West Coast Path? This is the description taken from the SWCP Association web site:

*The South West Coast Path itself is 630 miles long and is the longest National Trail in the country. Starting at Minehead in Somerset it runs along the coastline of Exmoor, continuing along the coast of North Devon into Cornwall. It follows the entire coastline of Cornwall, goes across the mouth of the River Tamar and continues into Devon. After running along the south coast of Devon it then follows the Dorset coastline before finally ending at Poole Harbour. Although the Coast Path is usually described in this anti-clockwise direction, from Minehead to Poole, this is purely convention and there is no reason why it cannot be walked in the opposite direction. It is well signed in both directions.*

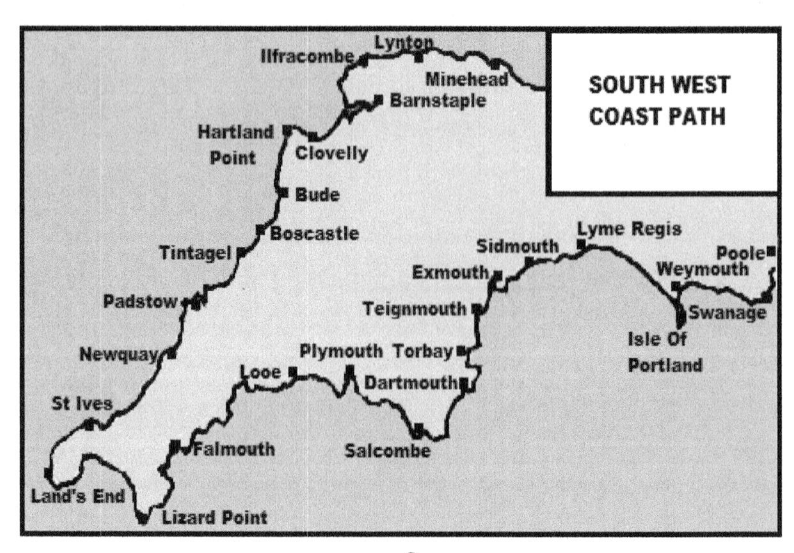

This well signed path uses the National Trail symbol of the acorn on its signposts hence the title of this book.

There are various reasons people choose to walk this path. Mine were threefold, the challenge, the experience and the scenery. Others may do it for the vast variety of wildlife, the geology, the heritage or any combination of all these things.

What you soon find out though is that "path" is a very loose generic term. The SWCP is any random combination of the following you could find yourself walking on. A narrow pathway cut into a hillside or a cliff, a field, a bridleway, a wooden or stone staircase, a road or lane, a sandy or shingle beach, a river crossing by ferry or on foot, a clamber over rocks and boulders and very occasionally and unfortunately a bus ride. Walking in terms of the SWCP is also a rather generic term. This can also include clambering, climbing, crawling, jumping, limping, slipping, sliding, stumbling, toiling, trudging and occasionally wading. All this walking is undertaken at the mercy of the various types of weather we experience in England, even in summer. During my walk this included torrential rain, a mini heat wave, dense fog and gale force winds.

# PROLOGUE

So who am I? Well this isn't an autobiography because it would be pretty boring and the early years are the chapters I sometimes skip when reading them. I do though want to tell you a little bit about my background to maybe understand how I got to this point in my life. I was born in Hove which is on the coast next door to Brighton where I spent most of my early life growing up and going out. I wasn't the greatest pupil in the world and went to an all-boys secondary modern school where I spent most of my time playing football or playing truant. Both of which I got to be quite good at. It was the sort of school where if you turned up for lessons more than two days running, the other lads thought you were a keener and the teachers thought you were star pupil material. I did actually attend a lesson once where I was the only pupil. If you're wondering about the lack of parental control that's mainly because my mum died when I was about 7 and my dad worked away a lot. Myself and two older sisters were passed around a lot between aunties and other distant family who really weren't interested. I ended up in foster care at the age of 14. My foster parents were both very wonderful people especially my foster mum. They weren't rich but incredibly kind and generous. They rarely had two pennies to rub together but when they did they would offer them to you. Most school lessons just got in the way of playing football apart from the two I actually liked, English Language and History. We didn't do English Literature as it was probably considered way beyond our intellect. I'm not sure why I liked these two subjects apart from the fact both involved writing essays which I thoroughly enjoyed. Well, I left school with two "O" levels, in English and History not surprisingly. I must have been interested in writing though because I did apply to the local paper for a job as a junior reporter but no joy. That I assumed was the end of my literary career and was the last time I did any serious writing. The only times I've really put pen to paper since then has been to fill out forms, prepare shopping lists or write on betting slips.

Let's fast forward about 40 years until about 2 years ago. I was on holiday in Cornwall when I first became aware of this path going up and down hills, close to the coast and people with rucksacks and camping gear walking along it. I also started to take notice of the coast path signs. After that I got more interested and did some research to find out some more. When I had found out the whole story it became a very definite ambition to walk this extraordinary path. I spoke to friends and work colleagues about it and they were also very interested and enthusiastic. The big difference was though they were talking about doing it in small chunks and camping along the way. My camping days were long over and that's if they ever began. I really do respect those campers especially the solo ones but I don't envy them. If I was going to do it I wanted to do the whole walk in one go and stay in bed and breakfast accommodation. Of course that isn't easy when you've got a full time job, so I guess it was put on my mental back burner probably until retirement which was still a few years away. Not many employers will give you 8 weeks leave, unless of course they're going to make you redundant.

Fast forward another 2 years and that is exactly what happened to me in March 2017. This was the second time this has happened to me in my working life. The first time was under very different circumstances but turned out to be a blessing in disguise. I was hoping history would repeat itself so felt quite ambivalent when I was given the news. I'd only worked there for a few years, but it was still a tidy enough redundancy pay off that I didn't have any immediate financial worries. I have to admit my first thoughts weren't "oh brilliant, I can walk the SWCP now". In fact, it wasn't until a couple of weeks later when watching the film "A Walk in the Woods" based on a Bill Bryson book, that I started thinking about it again. It was my partner Tonia who suggested that now would be a good time to do it. This did surprise me a little as it meant I was going to be away from home and her for 8 weeks...hmm I thought. However, I now had the time, resources and support for this amazing adventure so I started to look into all of it with much more serious intent.

**PREPARATION**

I went on the SWCP Association's website and started to do some planning. There is a stack of information on it including a suggested itinerary for walking the whole path over an eight week period, so that is what I decided to follow. With hindsight, I would probably do it differently. Some of the days were too short and I could have condensed it a little and saved myself some time and money. I didn't specifically want to do it on my own and had some good friends who would have loved to have come with me. They just couldn't get away for that length of time and at no small cost either. I did though have some offers to come and walk with me at different times over the eight weeks, for which I was very grateful. I split the walk into two halves of 26 days and built in a week's break. This was the school summer half term when I thought that the path would be busy and accommodation more expensive. The first half was to be from Monday 1$^{St}$ May beginning at Minehead in Somerset to Friday 26$^{th}$ May ending at The Lizard in Cornwall. The second part was from Monday 5$^{th}$ June recommencing at The Lizard until Friday 30$^{th}$ June ending at South Haven Point in Dorset. Of course staying

in B&Bs gets expensive and although I had the funds available it definitely wasn't a case of money being no object.
My strategy was to find the cheapest accommodation nearest to my finishing point on each day's walk and save money where possible by staying in Youth Hostels and Air B&B's. This seemed fine when booking it weeks before but more than a few times it bit me on the arse when staying in some of these places. There was a reason they were cheap: that was because sometimes they weren't very good and quite often way off the path. At the same time I also joined the SWCP Association and received an official guide book which was to become my bible. A whole stack of useful info is in this booklet and it's easy to carry around. The only thing I wasn't keen on was their directions which seemed rather vague. I needed something much more specific e.g. "take 3 steps forward and turn right" or "stop when you get to the cliff edge". The Association does provide individual walking guides with more detailed instructions but there were over 70 of these and at £2 a pop, costs would start to spiral. So, I opted instead for five A-Z Adventure Maps which bought as a pack cost me about £35. I also around that time joined a SWCP Facebook group. I was a very infrequent Facebook user but thought it would be a good idea to "talk" to people with knowledge and experience of this great walk and so it proved. I received a lot of responses to my request for advice and tips although at times it was a little conflicting. One of the main subjects which divided opinion was about the use of walking Poles. This has always been a divisive topic and since Brexit has become an even more contentious subject. I read all the posts but decided in the end not to use them. There was also lot of discussion about protecting your feet and legs from the rigours of strenuous walking every day. I was hopeful that as an experienced long distance runner both would be up to the test. A few people also expressed an interest in following my progress and asked for daily updates. I think I may have been one of the first contributors who were actually walking the entire path in one hit as it were. I was happy to report my progress but wasn't quite sure what they wanted to know. I also set up a WhatsApp

group at the suggestion of other friends and family called "Where's John" to keep in touch and send pics.
So, after gradually getting myself sorted with accommodation it was time to get some walking gear. I purchased what I hoped would be a good pair of comfortable and crucially waterproof boots, a large 60 litre rucksack, walking trousers, waterproofs and some merino socks. Coupled with a waterproof ski jacket I already possessed and a few other bits and pieces I thought I was the dogs' doo dahs. My mantra was very much "let's get ready to ramble"! How sadly naïve I was. As the saying goes, "all the gear, no idea" Although there were a few days along the way when it felt more like "all the wrong gear, stupid idea". In the early planning days though I was very enthusiastic and greatly looking forward to the whole experience up until about a week to go. Then I started to get cold feet even with both pairs of my merinos on. I guess the enormity of what I was taking on was starting to dawn on me. Day after day of long walks, on sometimes very difficult and testing terrain on my own without really knowing where I was going. Arriving hopefully in what to me would be strange places and sleeping in a different bed each night. I confess to being a little apprehensive on the drive from Bristol down to Minehead on the Sunday afternoon prior to starting. What didn't help either was the fact that the brilliant spring weather of April had broken. It rained on the way down there, during the evening and all through the night. I didn't sleep well.

What follows is my South West Coast Path story:

I have included my original Facebook postings in *italics* for each day. These posts were mostly written in bullet point form. A few corrections and amendments have been made mainly to remove the typos and punctuation errors. I apologise in advance for any that remain. Underneath the original postings I have expanded my commentary on each days walk. My early postings were very short and looking at them again a few weeks later I knew I could add a lot to them. I was tempted to incorporate them with the update commentaries into one daily entry. This may have made them appear more polished and professional. However, I decided against this as I didn't want to lose the immediacy and authenticity of my thoughts and feelings. Most of these posts were on Facebook within an hour or two of my finishing the day's walks. For some unknown reason from Day 21 on I started to include a limerick to sum up each day's walk. I wasn't entirely sure what people would make of them but they became very popular and I have added some new ones to the early posts which didn't have any. I have also included details of my daily accommodation for information purposes. The distances I have quoted are the official ones from the SWCPA guide book apart from a few deviations where I have made my own estimations.

Ok, enough of this rambling...Let's get walking!!!

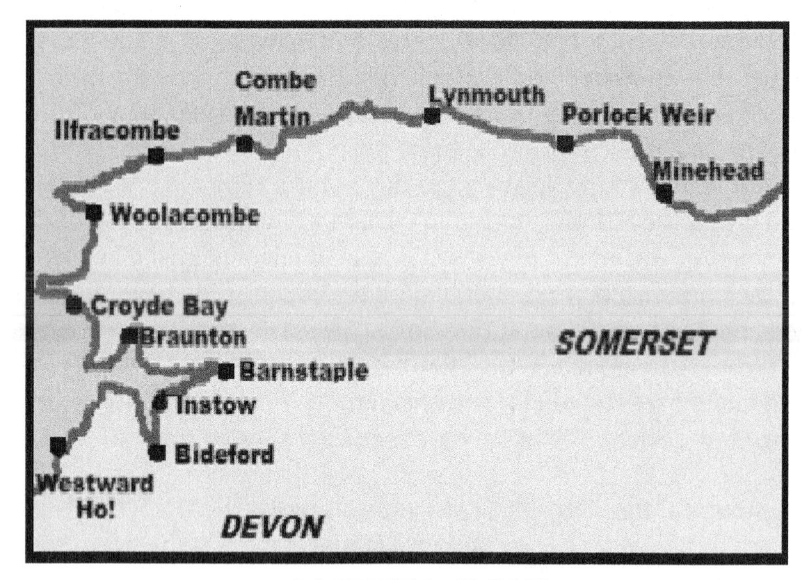


# WEEK ONE

Day 1

May 1$^{ST}$ 2017

Minehead to Porlock Weir – 9.3 mi [15.2km]

*After a night listening to torrential rain, it was a grey and dismal start to 8 weeks on the path. But after one small wrong turn it soon brightened up and by lunchtime the sun was shining. What a collection of contrasting terrain in this section. It had steep hilly coastal up and downs, but then lovely flat woodland and marshland. There was even a little jaunt over the beach to finish with. I loved it.*

As you can tell when I started posting I didn't really know what to write. I don't think Bill Bryson was losing sleep about any new competition. I kept it very brief and this is probably the way I thought it would continue. So let me tell you a little more about what happened that day. The rain had turned to a steady drizzle as I walked with Tonia to the celebratory starting [or ending] point marker on Minehead seafront. It was early on a wet bank holiday Monday so very quiet and empty. As we were taking the obligatory photos a voice from nowhere said "Do you want me to take one of you both?" We looked around to see this lady with short grey hair and of slight build in a jacket, shorts and carrying walking poles. She had walking shoes on, with what to me were weird things around them, which she later called gators. I'd heard of crocodile clips but gators? On her back was a miniscule looking backpack. She looked in her early to mid-60s and physically fit. We then returned the favour of a photo and got talking. She was English but had lived in New Zealand for the last 16 years. She had done various other long distance walks before in NZ, Australia and Spain. As we all started walking one of us suggested walking together and the other agreed. It did feel odd as I was all psyched up to being on my own and immediately I had agreed with this complete stranger to share my experience. Anyway after a brief kiss and goodbye embrace with Tonia off we went. It was only after a few miles that I stopped to think how Tonia might have felt seeing me wander off in the distance with a random unknown female. The first thing I noticed about walking with Lyn was that she was so bloody fast. I'm no slouch but she was a real shifter and I struggled initially to keep up. We talked a little as we walked but it soon became apparent that Lyn was quite a private person and I very quickly steered away from any real personal issues. I just managed to ascertain that she was single, no children, but still had relations in this part of the world and was retired from the NZ health service. She was also intending to walk the whole path and her itinerary for the first four weeks was identical to mine. She hadn't prebooked much accommodation and was looking to do that as she went along. It was a slow burning relationship which was to be expected but we got to be great friends. Of course it's difficult to talk face to face and walk at most times on the path when it's primarily single track. You get about as familiar with someone's back, bottom and legs as you do with their face especially when you're following them most of the time. I asked where the rest of her gear was and assumed she had arranged luggage transfers. She said "this is everything". Really, I wondered? I looked at her 3k backpack compared to my 10k rucksack and thought "one of us has got this seriously wrong". Then it sank in, that taking her experience of long distance walking into account versus my zero experience it was probably me! We were out of Minehead now but because we were talking we missed a sign, if there was one. That should direct you to North Hill above Burgundy Chapel not long after leaving the seafront. We just kept walking straight through Greenaleigh Farm to the Chapel remains. To correct this, we had to scramble up a steep slippery hillside to get back on track, which was exhausting. I had all my wet weather gear on anticipating a damp day and was absolutely drenched in sweat by the time I struggled to the top. It wasn't the most promising of starts, getting lost after the first mile. I distinctly recall thinking I hope the next 629 miles are not all like that. Anyway, after removing a few layers, on we went. It was soon apparent that Lyn's sense of direction was better than mine. I got better as the days went on, but Lyn hit the ground walking as it were in that respect. I remember feeling quite grateful for that and a little bit in awe. We then reached a point where you have a choice of paths. You can either walk the rugged seaward scenic one or the boring inland one. This is where we had a slight difference of opinion as Lyn had read that the rugged path adds an hour to the estimated completion time. On what was according to the guide book a short walking day that was fine by me. I always wanted to take the rugged path and Lyn was more convinced when a couple of local dog walkers also recommended it, so we did. It was a steep little path but not too difficult and with some great views out to sea [well, the Bristol Channel]. This is what I had come to the gig for! We then caught up with two young German girls who had stopped for a rest, not that we were chasing them I hasten to add. We stopped and had a chat. They were carrying an enormous amount of gear including a load of

camping equipment. They weren't the most robust looking of girls and I thought they might struggle with all that weight but it didn't seem to bother them. During the course of the entire walk I would quite often see young slightly built females with large rucksacks. It always made me feel a bit old and feeble. Shortly after this stop I recall the sun coming out and thinking this is more like it as we now got some great views out over the Channel from Hurlestone Point. We then went gingerly down a steep hilly descent and into the very pretty Bossington village. At this point something else happened that made me think that me and Lyn were going to get along. We passed a National Trust café that looked like a pub and we almost simultaneously suggested stopping for a pint. Unfortunately, the café didn't sell alcohol so we didn't but I distinctly remember thinking, ok, well at least the lady likes a drink. It later transpired that Lyn wasn't a big drinker but she did enjoy a post walk lager and maybe a glass of wine with a meal. We went our separate ways soon after as she was staying at a B&B in Porlock and I was booked into a hotel at Porlock Weir. We did agree to meet up the next morning though. It did initially seem a little odd to be walking alone but the sun was shining and I didn't have far to go and was really enjoying myself. I never mentioned Lyn in my early Facebook posts as she wasn't a member and I didn't want to be making comments "behind her back" as it were.
Crossing the marshland of Porlock Vale I came across a lady walking her dog. For the first but definitely not the last time as it was to happen quite often over the next few weeks, she asked me what I was doing. When I told her she said "Oh, I would have loved to have done that", to which my question as always was "what's stopping you now?" In this instance her response was very slow and she spoke with a real sadness in her eyes. Without going into detail she intimated she wasn't in good health. She wasn't old, but very thin and frail, so my assumption was she may have had something terminal. She said her husband would only be interested in walking the path if they camped everywhere, whereas in her condition she wouldn't be up to that. Her final words to me as she wished me on

my way were "perhaps he might consider it now with me having so little time left". I was quite upset and wanted to either throttle her husband for being so selfish or saying "sod him and come with me". I really hope he did take her. When I finally arrived at Porlock Weir I had conflicting feelings of satisfaction and anti-climax. It was only about 3 o'clock and I was thoroughly enjoying the day and felt like I wanted to go on. This is where prebooking accommodation has its drawbacks as you become a slave to your schedule. Once I'd had a pint though in the Ship Inn, looking over the pretty little harbour, I was very content. My only thoughts were what a lovely way it had been to spend and end a day.

*I walked the SWCP from Minehead to Porlock Weir*
*Before I started I was feeling just a touch of fear*
*But at the start I met a very nice lady called Lyn*
*And it turned into a great day for this adventure to begin*
*I then finished it off with a cold pint of beer*

ACCOMODATION - PORLOCK WEIR - MILLERS AT THE ANCHOR HOTEL. This is an interesting and quirky hotel. It's full of antiquities, stuffed animals and chandeliers in bathrooms.

Day 2

May 2ND 2017

## Porlock Weir to Lynton – 12.3mi [21.6km]

*Set off on a lovely morning but maybe underestimated this section. The first 3/4 is quite tough with some pretty severe ups and downs. Also, nearly all shaded woodland with occasional glimpses of the sea and coastline. There were a few other interesting bits along the way but not much. However, once you get around the last headland and get to look down on Lynton and Lynmouth it makes it all worthwhile.*

Another very brief post so let me expand on it a little. Lyn was a little late getting to join me at the Weir. Yesterday, when we had arranged to meet, I had thought the guest house she was staying at was a lot closer than it was. She eventually turned up about 9.30 on a sunny morning and mentioned she had found a little short cut to get to me. It was to be the first of many; Lyn did like to take a short cut. Not me, I much preferred shortcake. It did later get to be a long standing joke between us with me following official paths around headlands and the like and Lyn just wantonly cutting straight across them. She occasionally would be even naughtier and try to deliberately lead me astray if I wasn't paying attention. Off we set from the Weir and almost straightaway we were walking through woods and a good few miles of them. No sign of Tiger but lots of other wildlife. You get a few sightings of the sea but not many. This was never my favourite type of walking although Lyn being a nature lover was more enthusiastic. This was where we stopped for a brief chat with a chap who was typical of what I later used to refer to as a "white walker". This was a vague reference to Game of Thrones. In the programme white walkers are relentless killers. Obviously the SWCP walkers aren't killers but they sure like to murder the miles and they were definitely relentless. Heads down, poles out, taking long strides, they were usually campers with big rucksacks marching along barely looking up for signs. They appeared to me seemingly hell bent on racing to the finish with minimal enjoyment of the journey. This guy was in his 60s and was just finishing the path walking it the "wrong way" i.e. Poole to Minehead. It will have taken him about 30 days which meant he was walking on average over 20 miles a day. I was initially impressed but much less so the more I thought about it. It wasn't for me but we all do it in our own way and for our own reasons. A really welcome diversion in the woods was to Culbone Church which is the smallest parish church in England. There must have been a lot of atheists living in Culbone as it is tiny inside but well worth a visit. Once you emerge from the woods you are on high cliffs walking very close to the edge with much better sea views. This cliff top walking was not for Lyn as she didn't like it at all. This is where I would sometimes try to repay her efforts to "short cut" me by trying to "cliff edge" her into getting close and looking over. She never did. From there we walked on and around The Foreland and then the path goes on or close to the A39 road. Lynmouth and Lynton slowly come into view as the path zig zags down towards the foreshore. We stopped in Lynmouth at The Rock House to have what was to become our post walk ritual of two pints and two packets of crisps. Lynton sits on the top of Lynmouth separated by a steep cliff and connected by a funicular railway or the official route of a steep winding path. I was staying down in Lynmouth whilst Lyn had booked had accommodation up in Lynton and took the cliff railway to get there. Tut, tut, another short cut I muttered under my breath, like she ever cared. All of the three Lyn's were adorable. We never did come across Johnton or Johnmouth.

*I walked the SWCP to Lynton*
*After a trek through some woods it was a lovely walk in the sun*
*Stopped at a very small church along the way*
*Wouldn't be able to get more than a dozen people in there I would say*
*After the woods the walk was a lot more fun*

ACCOMODATION – LYNMOUTH - LORNA DOONE A really clean and comfortable good old fashioned Bed & Breakfast just up the Gorge.

Day 3

May 3RD 2017

Lynton to Combe Martin – 13.3mi [34.9km]

*Set off on a lovely sunny day. The first test of the day was the rather steep walk up from Lynmouth to Lynton. The cliff railway doesn't open until 10 o'clock so this wasn't an option.*

*I would recommend staying in Lynton to avoid the walk. The first 2-3 miles are superb. It's a nice flat path overlooking the sea and then some lovely grass tracks into the Valley of Rocks. Then it's a little more severe walking around some woods and on a road around Woody Bay. It started to get tougher then, up and down and around some headlands but spectacular views all the way. Then down and back up from Heddons Mouth which is quite testing and a few easier headlands and you reach the moors. There were lots of sheep grazing and it's an easier walk albeit a bit dull. You then see the Great Hangman in front of you and you know its trouble. After the long descent to the bottom of Sherrycombe you then go on the most leg stretching and lung busting climb of the path thus far. But at least the worst is now over. Continue over Exmoor and you get a glorious view of the coastline again with little Combe Martin in the distance. Carry on just a bit further to the Little Hangman and it's a lovely walk down to the beach. It took about 6 1/2 hours.*

This was a really enjoyable day's walk although quite tough especially towards the end. It included the first real big "un" of a climb in the shape of the Great Hangman which was an absolute beast. It has a fantastic start with the walk out towards Castle Rock in the Valley of Rocks on a high cliff path close to the edge. I used to love these cliff top walks as they always gave you the best sea views. I think it was about this time that I started noticing how many pictures I was taking compared to how few Lyn was. I would be snapping away like a frenzied Japanese tourist at Buckingham Palace and she would occasionally stop and take a photograph of...an orchid? The only orchid I was ever really interested in was Desert Orchid. We missed out on a couple of places along the way on this walk including Woody Bay and Hunters Inn which was a shame. They are not on the official path but not far from it. The Heddons Mouth valley was incredible though with a long winding descent to the valley floor then crossing over a stone bridge and back up the other very steep side. Then onto the Great Hangman which really is quite scary looking as it looms before you and is huge. I well remember a couple coming down as we were going up and stopping for a chat. I could hardly breathe let alone talk hence a lot of monosyllabic grunts in reply. Getting to the top was a huge relief and psychologically important as it is the highest point on the entire coast path. You then practically fall down the hill into Combe Martin and into the pub opposite the beach for more booze and crisps.

*I walked the SWCP to Combe Martin*
*From the Valley of Rocks is where this walk really gets starting*
*The Great Hangman in the distance is a sight to behold*
*The highest point on the whole path I've been told*
*What a scary place that would be to go extreme karting*

ACCOMODATION - COMBE MARTIN - FONTENAY B&B [also on AIR B&B]. This is different to your average B&B but very nice. The hosts live very much "the good life". There were a lot of examples of recycling going on which were very interesting.

Day 4

MAY 4TH 2017

## Combe Martin to Woolacombe - 13.6mi [21.9km]

*Most of the first part of this section to Ilfracombe runs alongside the A399 but the SWCPA seem to do their best to keep you away from the road and as near to the coast as possible. There are therefore some nice parts through woodland and fields to get you warmed up. Also very close to some cute bays and rocky coastline. You then have a steady walk down into Ilfracombe looking lovely in the sunshine after negotiating the quite steep circular route around a large mound called Hillsborough. Time then for a coffee and cake by the harbour where you can also gaze upon Verity which is the Damien Hirst statue looking out to sea. The path out of the town gets serious when it joins the Torrs walk around some largish headlands but with some dramatic coastline. Down into a pretty little place called Lee Bay and then you are in for some tough walking. The constant coastal views are amazing and then just when you're about done in, around a very rocky headland is Woolacombe looking all shiny and sandy. Great walk.*

This walk was the first one we had walked that was split into two halves by the SWCPA in their guide book. The first part was quite easy on the legs and pleasant as you make your way to Ilfracombe. Watermouth Cove can be crossed along a foreshore at most tides; we had to walk around it due to a high tide which was a shame. You only then get views looking back at it. From there it's down to a little beach at Hele just outside Ilfracombe and up and around Hillsborough. It's then a gentle descent into the town passing some large attractive Victorian houses and the charming harbour. Verity is interesting, grotesque and beautiful in equal measures on different sides. Finding our way out of Ilfracombe was a bit challenging as I recall. I often found the trickiest places to get out of were the busier towns. Once you do get out, you follow the Torrs Walk which is well waymarked but gets progressively tougher. Lee Bay is worth a stop with a nice café if you've not had enough to eat in Ilfracombe. There are some stunning views from there and unusual rock formations. Further on from there are a couple of steep valleys to overcome to reach a hill above Woolacombe on what was now a very warm day. You then look down and although you can't yet see it, you know somewhere down there is a bar with a cold pint waiting for you with your name on it. Should you happen to know Woolacombe, it was waiting in the Red Barn.

*I walked the SWCP to Woolacombe*
*It began by walking through woods with pretty flowers in bloom*
*Then a walk around Hillsborough and on the other side back down*
*I stopped for lunch in Ilfracombe; it's a busy little town*
*And finished the day off in the sunshine with a nice pint of Doom*

ACCOMODATION - WOOLACOMBE - THE BEACH HOUSE Very basic room with poor Wi-Fi. Breakfast was continental which means cereal and toast. Watch out for the toaster. It toasts your bread on one side with a flame thrower and the other with a hair dryer. If you like your toast black and white it's fine. I prefer mine in colour.

Day 5

May 5th 2017

Woolacombe to Braunton via Croyde Bay – 14.5mi [23.2km]

*This should have been quite a nice gentle short day but turned into something a lot more arduous. The walk began with a lovely stroll along Woolacombe Sands to start the day, with a bit of sunshine for company albeit a strong wind with it. You then walk up a hill and along to Baggy Point which is very close to the coastline and has great views out to sea. It's quite gentle in most places but when you turn the corner at the end don't miss the sign to the lower path. Nice easy walk then to Croyde Bay which has a large sandy beach. Stopped for a quick cuppa and a sarnie and then off to Braunton. It was an undemanding walk along by some rocky coastline. You then cross a road and go around Saunton Down with the glorious long Saunton Sands getting closer and closer. From here you have an option to go along the beach or up and over a hill to re-join the path a little further on. If you do take the upper path you will be rewarded with some fantastic views over the sands and the burrows and countryside. Then re-join the path and make your way through Braunton Burrows. Another flat walk through here on a good track but close to a golf course. Be careful to avoid any mishit golf shots and any misfires from the nearby military training area. Just here I made my first serious mistake of the trip and decided to take a short detour from the path. I wanted to get a closer look at the sand dunes and the beach. After consulting with a local who I later realised didn't know his "path from his elbow" I followed his directions and got very lost. I ended up walking a long way in all different directions surrounded by some angry looking cows and with rifle fire in the distance. I managed to get back to where I had come off the track but it took me over an hour. I later found out from some cyclists that I had been very badly misdirected by Mr Local. The rest of the walk then into Braunton is flat and follows the estuary. Nice coastal walk.*

This was another split day with the early morning walk across Woolacombe Sands very enjoyable. The alternative if the tide is high is to go through the dunes of Woolacombe Warren. That's never been a good option in my experience. There's usually a whole maze of different paths and it can be very taxing on the legs. I took this choice later in the afternoon with near dire consequences for me around Braunton Burrows. Got to Croyde Bay easily enough on a good path where we stopped at a holiday camp pub for an awful sandwich. Come the afternoon if you can walk along Saunton Sands then do so. The trudge through the burrows is long, flat and boring.

Once you're on them it's very difficult to get off as you can tell by my disastrous attempts above. Lyn didn't come with me when I went off to foolishly explore the sands. I told her I would be about twenty minutes and it was well over an hour. Even when I managed to negotiate my way out of the dunes I went walking in the wrong direction looking for her. Luckily, I came across some cyclists and asked them if they'd seen her which they had. They kindly went off to find her again and give her a message from me so we could meet up again, which we eventually did. She thought I'd been shot but that may have been wishful thinking. She never complained though, love her. I might have been just a bit peed off. From here is where the path then starts to follow the Tarka Trail, a former railway line and now a long narrow cycle track. It becomes very flat and frankly uninteresting. Because of my "detour" we were a little later than expected getting to Braunton and our beer and crisps.

*I walked the SWCP to Braunton*
*Along the way you pass by Saunton*
*It's better to walk along the sands if the tide's low*
*Walking through the dunes is long and slow*
*You'll also get very warm if you're under a hot sun*

ACCOMODATION – BRAUNTON - NORTH COTTAGE Another great old school B&B. Very reasonably priced with a decent pub just down the road.

Day 6

May 6th 2017

Braunton to Instow via Barnstaple – 12.6mi [20.2km]

*Today was a very easy flat walk. It didn't have quite the wow factor of previous days but was enjoyable enough. You pick up the path on the Tarka Trail which is a cycle path. No, I didn't know otters could cycle either but there you go. The trail takes you all the way to Barnstaple. It's a bit dull at first but soon opens up with nice views across the River Taw on one side and countryside on the other. After a quick stop in Barnstaple it's then over a lovely old bridge and back with Tarka up the other side of the river. I recommend a stop at Fremington Quay for a bite to eat. They serve very big tasty cakes. Back on the trail and the path takes you back along the riverside. Eventually though you will see Appledore across the river looking all cute and cuddly. On then you go to lovely little old Instow. It's very pretty with a sweet sandy beach and a quay full of all types of boats.*

No getting away from it really this whole Tarka trail bit is a little on the dull side. Nice and flat but all tarmac and hard on the feet. It includes a lot of urban walking and the majority of the views are from either side of the River Taw estuary or looking across the River Torridge. There's not a lot on show apart from sand and mud banks or water if the tide's in. I do realise though there are a whole lot of walkers out there with different styles and attitudes and some will probably love this walk. I didn't dislike it too much as you do get a chance of a breather for what's coming later on. I was quite keen on Instow as it's an attractive village. It has pubs, restaurants and some nice shops especially John's Delicatessen which did a great range of healthy food. There is another one in Appledore.

*I walked the SWCP to Instow*
*You follow a cycle path around the estuary and progress is slow*
*A stop at Fremington Quay for lunch is a treat*
*There's a great choice of tasty goodies on offer to eat*
*Appledore looked very pretty in the afternoon sun's glow*

ACCOMODATION – INSTOW - WAYFARER INN This is a pub right on the waterfront, its ok but nothing special.

Day 7

May 7th 2017

Instow to Westwood Ho! via Bideford – 11.7mi [18.8km]

*Back on the Tarka Trail this morning and very much like the last few miles. There are lots of fields on one side and the River Torridge on the other. It was a lovely sunny morning so pleasant enough but a bit samey. You cross the river over the old bridge and into little "priddy" Bideford. I stopped for a smoothie and had a look around before getting back onto the path. I was finally off the trail now but still by the river. It got a little more interesting with a walk around some fields and through woods and then into quaint looking Appledore. Strangely, I think it looked better from the other side of the river and so does Instow which you now look across to. Quick lunch stop in John's Delicatessen which I thoroughly recommend and onto Westward Ho! Probably the best part of the walk now around fields and burrows and always close to the sea. And then you reach Westward Ho. I have deliberately left off the exclamation mark as I don't think it deserves it. I felt somewhat underwhelmed; more like Westward Ho? or Westward So So. My least favourite day of the walk so far I think.*

This was the first day I actually did any walking on my own. Lyn had had enough of Tarka and his tarmac trail and decided to get the ferry from Instow to Appledore. I did of course point out that this was a massive cheat but she was never bothered. So we agreed to meet in Appledore about three o'clock which was when the first ferry was due to arrive. Ferries and tides were things that I never really factored in when planning the walk. I got lucky with them most of the time, apart from one notable exception in Falmouth, but you really do need to take them into consideration in planning. So off I went in the morning and just ambled along down the trail towards Bideford. Crossed the old bridge and then ambled back up the other side of the Torridge to Appledore. Lyn didn't really miss a lot. We met up again when the ferry came over. The path then improves a little as it takes you around Northam Burrows Country Park and into Westward Ho! via a golf course. It's a nice enough walk but there's not a lot to grab your attention. As you can tell, I didn't think much of the Ho! It was much too busy and commercial for my liking.

This was the end of the first week and it had been a very promising start. Apart from a couple of occasions the walking had not been too arduous but I knew there were much bigger challenges ahead. The weather had also been especially kind without any real sign of rain and generally sunny. I knew that couldn't last either but was very grateful while it did.

*I walked the SWCP to Westward Ho!*
*Stopped at Bideford where there's a statue of Charles Kingsley you know*
*There's not a lot else to remark upon along this way*
*Although it was pleasant enough on a sunny Sunday*
*I'm expecting after here there's a lot more on show*

ACCOMODATION – NORTHAM - AIR B&B. My first experience of Air B&B and a positive one. It was quite close to Westward Ho and also Appledore. It wasn't a large house or a big room but very clean and tidy. Alison the host was lovely and friendly. Tonia had come down to stay with me and Alison gave us a lift into Appledore in the evening and a little guided tour. She also made some very tasty porridge for breakfast and toast etc.

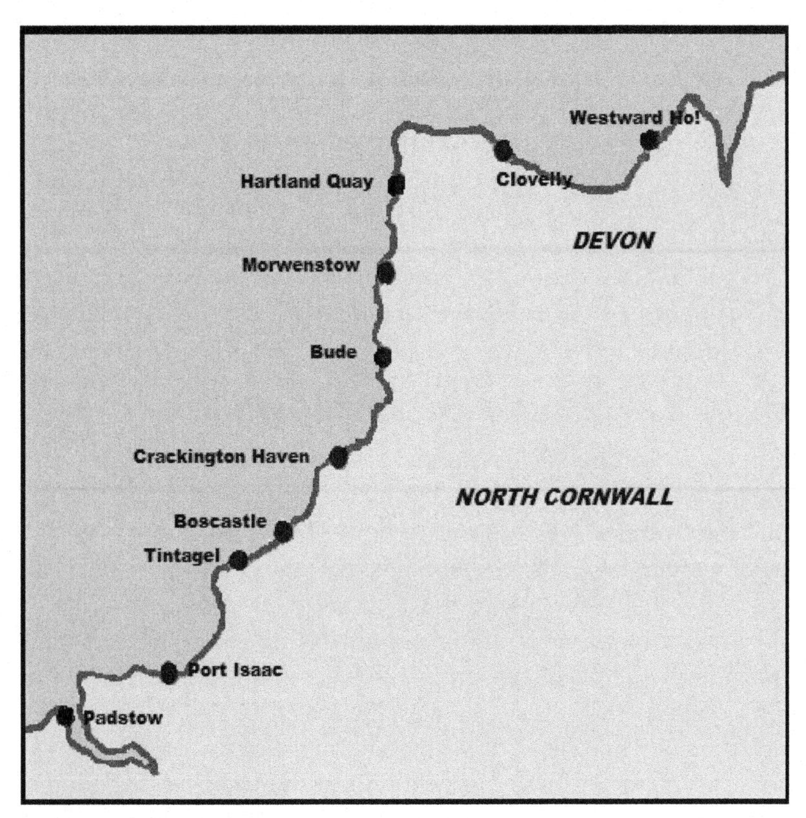


# WEEK TWO

Day 8

May 8th 2017

Westward Ho! to Clovelly – 11.2mi [18.0km]

*I left the town on a glorious morning, feeling so happy and lucky to be doing this and not at work on a Monday morning. It's a lovely walk to start with next to green fields and glistening blue sea. Good to be back on a proper path with lots of undulations after the flat banality of the last few days.*

*Some pretty isolated bays with the tide out exposing some smashing beaches. There is then a nice walk through woods with omnipresent bluebells for constant company. Then you come out of the woods to a little gem of a bay called Buck Mills. A little detour down to the beach is well worth it. Back into woods and trees and fields and more bluebells. Then you hit a long winding wooded road called The Hobby Drive. This takes you all the way down into Clovelly, the quintessential English fishing village. Unspoilt by modern culture and still using donkeys for carriage and the locals using sleighs to get their shopping down the incredibly steep hill. It's full of charming little cottages and shops and tiny harbour. Unique.*

I think I was a bit harsh in my initial assessment of Westward Ho! It looked a lot better in the morning with the tide out and nowhere near as crowded as yesterday afternoon. Met Lyn on the seafront and off we went. I really enjoyed this walk and to finish in Clovelly was a real delight. I had heard a little about it but never been so was really looking forward to seeing it for myself. We got there around mid-afternoon and I checked into the New Inn Hotel which is on the steep cobbled main street. It was most enchanting if somewhat antiquated but that all adds to the character of the whole village. Lyn was also staying there and we booked ourselves in for dinner. My room had a small balcony area with a view straight down the high street but the thing I remember most was a horrible stench when you used the sink. I decided I would go and have a quick wander around the village and made my way down to the small harbour to take a few pictures. I was trying to get a selfie but failing miserably. There was a young lady sitting in the sun and enjoying a glass of white wine. I asked her if she would take a picture of me which she did. We got talking a little, her name was Laura she was tall and thin and from the Midlands. Leggy Laura from Leicester as I later used to think of her. I asked what she was doing and she said that she was on a road trip around the South West for two weeks travelling alone. She had been to Bath and Bristol and was going on to Newquay the next day to get some surf lessons. She also happened to be staying at the New Inn. Lyn had arrived by now and I left them talking and went back for a shower. I went downstairs for dinner about seven and the restaurant area was already crowded. It was generally filled with other walkers staying there and a few locals, all middle to old aged. It had been a warm day and most people were very casually dressed in shorts, short sleeved shirts and similar attire. Not long after, Laura made her appearance. A lot of jaw dropping went on and the room fell very quiet. She was dressed to the nines in a long black designer evening dress looking a million dollars. She wouldn't have appeared out of place on the red carpet at a film premiere. Unfortunately, she was surrounded by a lot of older people in garb looking like thirty quid's worth from Marks and Sparks. To say that she was over dressed would be an enormous understatement. I felt a little sorry for her but she carried it off well and didn't seem too embarrassed. About an hour later the place was empty and I was tired so I left her chatting to the barman. I think she might have felt more at home amongst the surfers in Newquay.

*I walked the SWCP to Clovelly*
*It was a tough at times and my legs often felt like jelly*
*It was a delightful place for a final destination*
*Living in the past maybe but steeped in tradition*
*I just wish my hotel room hadn't been so smelly*

ACCOMODATION – CLOVELLY - NEW INN Genuinely olde worlde but try to avoid room seven if you can.

Day 9

May 9th 2017

Clovelly to Hartland Quay – 10.3mi [16.6km]

*This is a walk in three sections today. They were all enjoyable but becoming progressively more testing. The superb scenery also increased incrementally in its magnificence and the last section was just outstanding. You exit Clovelly via a steep walk up the cobbled main street, turn right at the top and are immediately back on the path. Just be careful not to miss a black gate otherwise you end up heading back down to a beach and it's a killer coming back up. I know because I did this, much to the amusement of a local passer-by who found it hysterical, which it definitely wasn't! Anyway a nice walk follows above some cliffs and over fairly flat fields with plenty of little bays and coastline to enjoy. Then down to a lovely little beach at Mouth Mill, over a stream and up and back on top of the high cliffs. If you like cliffs you're going to really love this stretch, Brownsham Cliff, Beckland Cliff, Jimmy Cliff, Cliff Richard and plenty more. Then there is a jaunt over two large bays and on to Hartland Point. After a quick refreshment stop and from here on, the fun really starts. This last section down to Hartland Quay is very steep in places but so worth the sweat. The most glorious rugged bit of craggy coastline so far and the views from up high are amazing. You eventually arrive about two hours later and a few pounds lighter at Hartland Quay; which is spectacular and a truly great end to the day.*

I got a decent night's sleep at the New Inn. On leaving the hotel and walking up the hill to get out of the village we passed a few locals. There was something about the look of them that I couldn't quite put my finger on but I'm sure I heard Duelling Banjos playing somewhere last night. Anyway, after getting carelessly lost within the first mile we were soon back on track and making good progress. This is the section of the path where you turn from going East-West to North-South at Hartland Point. It's also where the walking gets very serious but so does the spectacular coastline. There are big dark scary looking cliffs and from the beaches, slithers of rocks pointing out to the Atlantic. It also feels very remote and lonely. I was staying at an Air B&B in Hartland which is a couple of miles inland. It was a bit further than I had anticipated and I wasn't looking forward to the extra miles when I was sitting having the post walk ritual of a pint and crisps. Then a chap who was doing some gardening started chatting to us and when he found out where I was staying very kindly offered me a lift, result! He was a very friendly chap and we got on like a house on fire. I stayed at a small farm called Cheristow Lavender. I had a big room which was very clean and comfortable. The couple who own and run it are lovely. It is a traditionally run low impact beef farm. It also has a huge lavender garden out the back. Everything is grown organically. They also have a small tearoom there which is open to the public, again all the food is organic and homemade. I was given a cream tea when first I got there which was absolutely scrumptious. They asked if I wanted to join them for dinner which they did charge for but which I was more than happy to accept. It was Beef Wellington with all organic vegetables and was delicious as was the homemade sticky toffee pudding for afters. The only small downside was halfway through the main course they were telling me that they name every animal they rear and eat their own livestock. This evening we were enjoying the dearly departed Devon Red Ruby cow previously known as Buttons. I did nearly choke on my mouthful of beef at the time but all I can say is Buttons my late friend, you were extremely succulent. In the morning I had eggs and bacon courtesy of Jemina and Percy.

*I walked the SWCP to Hartland Quay*
*Don't miss the black gate out of Clovelly or you'll end up in the sea*
*When my walk had come to an end*
*I had a lift to my accommodation from my new best friend*
*And ended the day having Buttons for tea*

ACCOMODATION – HARTLAND - CHERISTOW LAVENDER B&B [also on AIR B&B] In a lovely rural setting, nice big comfortable room. Very good food providing you don't mind eating something you probably walked past on the way in.

Day 10

May 10th 2017

Hartland Quay to Bude – 15.4mi [24.8km]

*Well this was it, the Big One, The Whopper! Officially it is 15.4 miles and an estimated 8 1/2 hours of severe walking with ten [yes, that's ten] extremely steep river valley crossings. Well after the initial few miles I was wondering what all the fuss was about. Strolling along it was all lovely jubbly, easy peasey lemon squeezy. I'll be on the beach in Bude for lunchtime topping up the tan with a nice cold one for company. Err, wrong! Get to Welcombe Mouth and the river valley roller coaster kicks in. Scream if you wanna go steeper.*

*Bang, bang, bang, bang, bang, five of the monsters! Deep zig zagging, slippery slopes going down that were so deep I swear I thought my toes were going to burst through the tops of my boots at any time. Then you go over a small bridge and up very steep paths where just when you think you've reached the top, they get higher. You also have to deal with those bloody great big wooden steps that were surely designed for the BFG. My calves have doubled in size today and I could barely get my jeans on over them tonight. But it is so worth it. The coastline is just staggeringly spectacular. After a short break and detour near Morwenstow it's back on the ride and four more river crossings. Finally after the last one it's a wonderful walk on top of the cliffs above some beautiful beaches and down into Bude. I couldn't resist a paddle in the sea on the big sandy beach. I definitely recommend that as a way to cool down the feet. It was a truly memorable walk. It's tough but you've got to do it!*

This was definitely one of my favourite days of the entire walk. The beginning does lull you into a false sense of complacency, but when it starts it is relentless and incredibly challenging. Every one of those river crossings had huge ups and downs. They drag out every last gasp of breath from your lungs and stretch every sinew in your legs. Lyn decided to bail out at Morwenstow after we had something to eat at the café there. This surprised me a little because I thought she was doing really well up to that point but she always did know her limitations. She also never worried about leaving out pieces of the path here and there. I continued alone back on the roller coaster and eventually struggled and sweated my way to Bude. Despite the difficulty I thoroughly enjoyed it and had a massive sense of achievement when I'd finished. I had taken on what many consider to be the hardest stretch of this path and smashed it, well, maybe not smashed it, more like slightly squashed it. I was also extremely hot and when my feet hit that sea water you almost hear the hiss and see the steam coming off them. I've never enjoyed a paddle so much in my life and still don't know to this day why I didn't have a swim. Not long after, I left to find my accommodation which was a pub close to the beach. That first pint didn't touch the sides and the second barely skimmed them.

*I walked the SWCP to Bude*
*To get there, a very difficult path over many large hills is pursued*
*At half way there is a welcome stop at Morwenstow*
*Up to this point the going is gruelling and slow*
*When I'd finished I was in a very chilled mood*

ACCOMODATION - BUDE - BRENDON ARMS PUB Very central and right on the path. You don't want to have far to go when you've finished this walk. The rooms were clean and comfortable.

Day 11

May 11th 2017

Bude to Crackington Haven – 10.2mi [16.4km]

*Well this little fella had a right sting in its tail! A nice steady walk out of a warm cloudy Bude along the cliff top to begin with. After my misguided complacency yesterday morning I wasn't taking anything for granted. However, it was easy on the eye and easy on the legs and feet which both appreciated. The coastline was a continuation of the same rocky rugged beaches that were so prevalent further up the coast but less spectacular. After about another three miles you arrive at Widemouth Bay. This is a large sandy beach and things get a bit more serious from here with a steep road climb up to Penhalt Cliff but with a super view for your efforts. Then you walk across a field to a very steep descent to Milook Haven. You climb back up to a few fields to cross along more cliffs. It gets very serious hereafter with two very deep and steep valley crossings which were on a par with yesterday and definitely knocks the stuffing out of you. A rather narrow ridge walk takes you out to Castle Point which wouldn't be for the faint hearted on a windy day. Then you reach the last, but not the least, of the valley crossings. This one takes you on an extremely long leg stretching trek back up more giant steps to Pencannow Point. It's one of those climbs where you look back and see the path snaking down and then back up again and wonder how the hell you did it. But you did and you can finally relax and look down on Crackington Haven. Nice gentle walk down and a pint to savour. Cheers!*

This was a relatively short walk of just over ten miles. It's another one where depending on your viewpoint the best or worst is saved for last. I have to admit to wanting to get the tough stuff out of the way early on so you could relax a little and enjoy it more. I was never of the opinion where unless there are a lot of hills to test you, a walk is dull and boring. I liked the variety of the terrain on different days and the diversity of difficulty. There was plenty of hard walking days so a few gimmes thrown in were also welcome providing they were still interesting. I vividly recall a thin fit looking chap in a Juventus football shirt attempting to run up that last hill to Pencannow Point. I stopped to see how far he could possibly get and watched in amazement as he actually made it all the way to the top! Strange, I always believed that Mo Farah was an Arsenal fan. Crackington Haven is small and quiet but with a decent pub and a couple of cafés right near the beach. Myself and Lyn were both booked into a B&B in a place called Higher Tresmorn which was about two miles away. If I'd been on my own I probably would have walked as we had finished quite early, but Lyn was having none of it. There was no mobile signal available, so she borrowed the land line phone from the café and rang the host leaving messages for her. These were along the lines of "please come and get us because it's too far to walk". We probably had to wait about two hours before eventually she came and picked us up but was definitely not overly impressed about being summoned by Lyn. Naturally of course, Lyn also insisted on her taking us back down again to the beach in the morning. They've got some nerve those Kiwis.

*I walked the SWCP to Crackington Haven*
*Some of the hills to walk over have extremely high elevation*
*The walk wasn't especially long*
*If I said it took about five hours I wouldn't be far wrong*
*My B&B host provided some transportation*

ACCOMODATION - HIGHER TRESMORN - HIGHER TRESMORN FARM B&B It was comfortable accommodation on a small farm. A three course evening meal is also possible on request which we had as the farm is rather isolated. Owner may be prepared to pick up and drop off.

Day 12

May 12th 2017

Crackington Haven to Tintagel – 11.4mi [18.3km]

*This was a real day of two halves. Both were memorable but for completely different reasons. The morning was spent walking to Boscastle and the afternoon to Tintagel. You're on the rise straight from the off on this one and apart from a couple of flattish cliff top areas it's almost all up and downers to Boscastle. Almost immediately you are zig zagging up a headland called Cambeak and wishing you hadn't had that extra slice of toast for breakfast. A flat stretch follows but pretty soon you see High Cliff and it's not called High for any reason. To be fair the ascent isn't too bad but the descent is one of those where you really think you're going to need a parachute to get to the bottom. The saving grace is some good steps going down which really do help. A long winding climb back up but with a bench perfectly placed for a rest stop at the top. Then on along the cliff tops through fields which gives you some valuable breathing space. You pass by a massive sheer black rock called Buckator which really stands out and looks a real brute. After this is Fire Beacon Point before you begin to go down again and carefully along a narrow path to a waterfall called Pentargon. The first part of the descent is down some very steep almost vertical slate steps. If you have a fear of heights or cliffs edges and it's blowing a real hooley which it was today, than it's really squeaky bum time. After that it's gentler and takes you on pass Pentargon. You start to notice a change in the coastline here from the rocky shores and sandy beaches to cliffs that drop straight down into the sea. A stiff walk over the bridge and up the other side of the waterfall is the last big ask of this section before you get to Boscastle Harbour. A stop for a cuppa and I thought rather appropriately a rock cake, then off to Tintagel. I was really looking forward to this section. It was described as a moderate walk of about 2.25 hours and apparently combines all the best aspects of the coast path apart from one vital thing...the weather. In the morning it had been humid and overcast with occasional sunshine and some drizzle. That was how it was for the first couple of miles and a really good walk too. Not easy but a great coastline coming out of the harbour and very pleasant countryside. Then it started to rain. Just more drizzle at first but instead of dying out it just got heavier and heavier and wetter and wetter. At the same time the wind was also getting up a head of steam. The good weather gods that had looked after me for the last 11 days had decided I'd been spoilt, now the bad weather gods were about to extract a terrible revenge. I'd just reached Rocky Valley and got all my wet weather gear on and it absolutely poured down. Sheeting rain and howling wind just descended and within about ten minutes I wasn't walking on a path anymore; I was wading and squelching my way over a fast flowing muddy stream. Slipping and sliding over slate stones that in the dry are great to walk on but when wet are treacherous. Anyway, all I could do was just keep my head down and follow the stream. Occasionally I put it up to try and see what I was missing but never for long. It was miserable and when I got to the village I had another mile to walk in to my B&B. I guess at least I found out what gear I had was waterproof: None.*

Today was the day I knew was coming so shouldn't have been surprised. After eleven days of dry, sunny and at times hot weather, the rains came. When it rains on the coast path you are stuffed. You have no shelter and are completely exposed. Usually with the rain comes the wind which just makes it so much worse. I honestly don't mind getting wet but this sort of wet was on a different scale. The most disappointing aspect of it was the almost total failure of my gear to keep me at least a little dry. My boots were especially useless. They weren't cheap but I definitely regretted not spending more to try and get some with better wet weather protection. They were very comfortable and in the dry were fine but when it rained they were about as much use as a chocolate teapot. The other really annoying thing is that the weather almost completely disables you from being able to see anything. There was a large section of this walk that I missed and that is frustrating. I didn't want to be seen as a fair weather walker. Most people who have walked this wonderful path will have at some point been caught in the rain. You just have to put your hood up, head down, accept it and get on with it.

*I walked the SWCP to Tintagel*
*You pass through Boscastle on the way as well*
*There was a waterfall I passed which was a sight to adore*
*I would have liked to have seen a lot more*
*But when the rains came it wasn't a place to dwell*

ACCOMODATION – TINTAGEL – TREKNOW B&B [also on AIR B&B] It was ok, I had a very small en-suite room but everything was there, just in miniature. I did feel a bit like Gulliver.

Day 13

May 13th 2017

Tintagel to Port Isaac – 9.1mi [14.7km]

*I'm not really a superstitious person but after yesterday's washout and it being Day 13 I wasn't taking any chances. I was touching all the wood I could find, being very careful around mirrors and definitely not walking under any ladders. Although to be honest I've not come across many window cleaners on the path. After having a day off the good weather gods were back at work and it was a gloriously sunny start to the day in Tintagel. It gave me the opportunity to see at least some of what I missed yesterday and wow, what a bit of coastline that is by the castle remains where the walk restarts. Very rocky rugged coastline and with a much stronger wind than recently whipping up the waves, it was a great sight. Fairly gentle to start with as the path takes you out and around Penhallic Point with superb views out to the Atlantic. One of the main features of this walk is the sight of Port Isaac glowing in the distance from a very early stage. It constantly teases you with its proximity but don't be fooled, it's a long old way. Early on is the first challenge on a day which was to prove very challenging, this was the climb up some very big, steep steps from Trebarwith Strand. They really should carry a government health warning. It does have a gorgeous beach at the bottom though with a few facilities. Almost immediately you're having to go back down and up again at Backways Cove. A little respite on a long level stretch and then the rollercoaster starts again with a triple whammy of three big dippers. All very similar in their degree of difficulty but made harder by some very tricky underfoot conditions on the descent. Real lung busting whoppers these are as they just seem to go on and on and up and up and up even more. Great looking back at them though when you eventually get your breath back. The worst is out of the way now with just one smaller but not much easier valley to cross at St Illickswell Gug. The path then levels off and takes you through some cliff top meadows. This whole section was probably the most overgrown path I've walked thus far. Because of the weather I was in shorts and it was quite painful at times with a lot of nettles and gorse prevalent. On then to Port Gaverne which was very pretty, up a short hill to a car park and down into Port Isaac harbour. It was a really testing but enjoyable walk with almost constant views of the superb Cornish coastline.*

I managed to get most of my gear dry overnight using a combination of a convector heater, a hair dryer and the large radiator outside my bedroom. Had an early breakfast and set off in much better spirits than when I'd finished yesterday's walk. I walked this section on my own as Lyn had accommodation problems around Port Isaac and had to make other arrangements but with plans to re-join me in Padstow in a couple of days. She did actually walk this leg, but on her own as she was setting off at silly o'clock in the morning. This was my first complete day walking on my own and I was slightly apprehensive. It turned out to be an easy walk to follow although physically very challenging in places but thoroughly rewarding. Port Isaac was very crowded no doubt with many Doc Martin fans. I spent some time there in the afternoon as I couldn't book into my B&B until four o'clock. Bed and breakfast accommodation is very expensive around this area probably due to the Doc Martin effect. It's especially difficult at weekends where you are expected to book for a minimum two nights. I got lucky in that respect as I managed to find a smart B&B run by a super couple at a very reasonable price. It is in small village called Pendoggett [love that name, it's so Poldark] which is a 1 ½ miles away but the owner will pick you up and drop you back in the morning to Port Isaac car park.

*I walked the SWCP to Port Isaac*
*Some of the scenery leaving Tintagel left me quite awestruck*
*My destination was easy to see in the distance*
*But as it only got slowly closer I almost doubted its existence*
*I was hoping to see Doc Martin but was out of luck*

ACCOMODATION – PENDOGGETT - LANE END FARM B&B Extremely comfy and very Cornish. Nice rooms and extremely reasonably priced for this area. Good pub down the end of the lane called The Cornish Arms.

Day 14

May 14TH 2017

Port Isaac to Padstow – 11.7mi [18.9km]

*Left Port Isaac on a rather cloudy but breezy day but the sun soon came shining through. The village was eerily empty and quiet but seemed very peaceful with the tide in and a few boats bobbing about in the harbour. This was quite a contrast from when I arrived yesterday afternoon when it was rammed with tourists and presumably Doc Martin devotees. I know the show must have brought prosperity to the commercial interests of the place but the local born and bred residents must have misgivings. You leave here with a nice walk up the hill with great views looking back. Then you drop down quite sharply to Pine Haven and a double set of steps, which are even steeper going back up which I really wasn't expecting so early in the proceedings. Because of the previous day's rain the path was very slippery in parts and I came a right Roy Cropper a few times today. Then it's a winding undulating path all the way to Port Quinn. Take a walk out to Varley Head for some great views out to sea and more of that glorious Cornish coastline. Port Quinn is a lovely little place. A kind of mini version of Port Isaac before the tourists invaded. A steepish walk up a hill takes you out to the folly of Doyden Castle on Doyden Point. Again I would encourage a walk out to the end of the Point for some superb coastal scenery. Then a flattish walk before another very slippery descent to Epphaven Cove which I thought was a delightful little spot with a small beach. Then the path takes through some woods before rising up again for a smashing stretch of path out to The Rumps headland. The bluebells were out in force again after being mainly absent for the last couple of days. A lot of little coves along this stretch and very green. When you get to The Rumps once again a small diversion out to the Point will be well rewarded. If like me you're wondering why it's called The Rumps it will become apparent and impressively so. On from there and around Pentire Point and the walking gets easier but the views are still breathtaking. Polzeath and its fabulous beach are soon in view. There were a lot of people out on the path today more than at any time previously so far. One stopped me and asked me something I've never been asked before. "Have you seen any puffins on your walk?" I replied" Well, I've seen a few people" puffin" but not sure she understood. The surf was up at Polzeath so I got my board out and did a few high fives, roly polys and hang overs. Then back on the path to Daymer Bay, a lovely long stretch of beach that extends all the way to Rock. As it was low tide I was able to walk all the way on magnificent golden sweeping sands. I had views of the sand dunes one side and views across to Padstow on the other. At low tide little sand islands form and you can jump from one to another and go quite a long way out. So I did. Seems a little childish now but was great fun at the time. Then back on dry land/sand and on to Rock. Home to the world famous and terrifically named sandbank called The Doom Bar. What a great beer! Astonishingly, neither of the bars right by the ferry jetty were selling it. They make the lovely stuff just up the road! So I got on the ferry to Padstow and straight in the nearest boozer for a pint to complete what was one of the best days of this adventure so far.*

This was a really great day and a marvellous walk. I was on my own again as Lyn had a two night stopover in Padstow. What I didn't include in my original post was the few extra miles I walked after getting to Padstow. I was staying with Tonia's mum who lives in Wadebridge. I had intended getting a bus but was enjoying the day so much I decided to walk there along the Camel trail. It's about five miles and a lovely walk on the cycleway alongside the River Camel estuary. I was a little tired when I eventually got there but Celia looked after me very well.

*I walked the SWCP to Padstow*
*A fantastic walk with so much beautiful scenery on show*
*There are a lot of very big steps just after the start*
*But is easier from Lundy Point which is about the middle part*
*And jumping around sand islands in Rock was great fun you know*

ACCOMODATION – WADEBRIDGE - TONIAS MUM Best landlady ever but sadly this accommodation is not available to the general public.

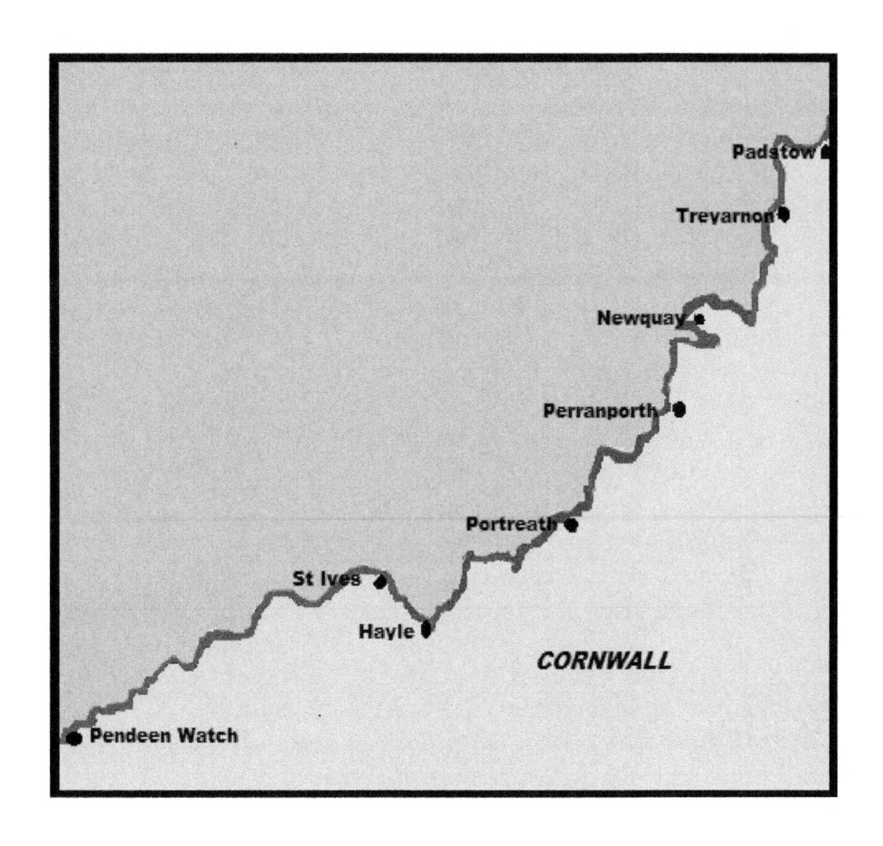


# WEEK THREE

Day 15

May $15^{TH}$ 2017

Padstow to Treyarnon – 12.1mi [17.65km]-my estimate

*As I'm walking, different song titles or lyrics pop into my head prompted by whatever might be happening at the time. Today's song titles were "What A Difference A Day Makes", "Blowing In The Wind" and "I Can't Stand The Rain".*

*Set off from Padstow under grey leaden skies, persistent drizzle, low mist and a high tide. A nice gentle walk takes you out to a great beach area called Hawkers Cove. As you walk along this coastline you are looking across the river at yesterday's walk from Daymer Bay to Rock. No sign today of The Doom Bar and if I followed the same route over the sand where I walked yesterday I would probably be under six foot of water. You then go up a steepish climb to Stepper Point and turn left towards an old lookout station. Or at least you try to. This is where the Atlantic headwind really goes into overdrive and it's like someone's turning on a giant hair dryer at full blast in your face. Because of the weather I had my rain cover on over my ruck sack and I swear it nearly made it and me take off. Due to this headwind from here on you can only walk very slowly. There are some great views inland and to your right the very steep rugged cliff formations are amazing. It was very, very tempting to get as close to the cliff edge as you can to get a full view but be very, very careful if there's a strong headwind like today. You then follow the cliffs round into Trevone which has an attractive narrow beach area. A nice café gives you a chance to have a rest and put your hair straight. Any wig wearers out there might want to think twice about walking this bit of path. There follows a really nice length of path which takes in the best that Cornwall has to offer the beach and bay lover. Real picture postcard pretty this area. Harlyn Bay onto Mother Ivy's Bay is fabulous with a number of smaller and secluded beaches along the way. They maybe weren't looking quite as resplendent as they would have yesterday but their golden shine even under a murky backdrop was dazzling. You also get to see the Padstow lifeboat station and then walk on to Trevose Head passing a lighthouse. That's when my luck with the weather ran out. Up to this point it had been miraculously dry, but turning on the path back towards more glorious beaches the wind really got up and the rain started to sweep in off the Atlantic. It wasn't torrential but definitely hoods up time. You then pass a strange rocky Boobys Bay [quick snigger] and on to Constantine Bay. The surf was really up now and it was an awe inspiring sight watching the waves crashing in on the beach. The path takes you across the beach and then up and around to Treyarnon Bay. This is where my walk finished for the day as I was staying in the YHA there. I was quite pleased as the rain had really set in by then. Will pick the path back up tomorrow and pass Porthcothan on the way to Newquay.*

This is an area of Cornwall that I'm more familiar with as Tonia grew up around here and we've been back here a few times and walked the coast path without ever realising it. I remember vividly walking from Harlyn to Mother Ivy's Bay on a glorious summer's day, a little bit different today but still a great walk. There are many people who come on holiday to Cornwall and know of the more famous and popular beaches but they are of course also the most crowded. What I didn't quite comprehend until this walk was just how many there are along this coastline in particular. Every time you moved on from one there was another. Some aren't easily accessible but if you want some seclusion away from the holidaying masses, you don't have to look too hard to find them, but you will have to walk to them. Today was also my first experience in my life of an YHA. The one at Treyarnon is very smart having had a very expensive refurbishment recently. It was the only one I stayed at that was open all day and had a proper little restaurant and bar. I enjoyed my stay here and slept ok, regrettably that was probably the one and only time I did get a decent night's sleep in an YHA. In principle they are great for walkers and backpackers. They are cheap, clean and comfortable with a kitchen area for you to prepare your own food, a lounge area and showers. They also have drying rooms which are a godsend if it's been a wet day or you need to wash and dry clothing. The first thing that struck me about them and was a recurring impression was the actual age of the guests. I was expecting especially in this red hot surfing location to find a lot of young surfing dudes hanging out. Well I never saw one, not here or in any of the half dozen I stayed in. In fact, it was the complete opposite. I think the average age of residents was probably about 50. Youth

Hostel Association? More like Youth Hostile Association I mused. This was also the first time I came across a character I called Smelly Don. He was an American gentleman in his early 70s who adored the SWCP and came over every year for about a month to walk the path. He was a likeable, amiable chatty gent and he was sharing my dormitory. However, it soon became apparent that Don had two very unattractive personal traits, an almost total lack of hygiene and to put it politely: thriftiness. To put it impolitely, he was as tight as a ducks arse. This was a man who was retired and took his wife on holidays to Florence and Paris and played the stock market. He definitely gave the impression that he wasn't short of a bob or two, but Don would never spend a bob if a sixpence would do. He always stayed in YHAs or very cheap B&Bs. He would go the local shop or supermarket and buy all the food they sell off very cheaply at the end of the day. If he had to eat out he loved Wetherspoons because in his words "you get a free drink with your meal". I once overheard him telling someone about how this frugalness had been instilled on him by his father. Well Don, from what I witnessed, you would have made your old man very proud. He travelled very light which I asked him about once. His philosophy was to bring all his nearly worn out underwear and socks. He would then wear them until they literally disintegrated and only then would he get rid of them. Either that or they were so alive with germs they walked off on their own. Our paths crossed a few times and I never saw him in any other clothes other than a black top, shorts and the most disgustingly discoloured "white" socks full of holes. I also never saw him wash any of his clothes or himself for that matter. Lyn once spent a very uncomfortable time sat near to him in a lounge with Don lying with his feet up on the seat next to her in his pungent holey socks. You could smell them from the other side of the room. She could be quite a forthright lady and told me later she was very close to having words. I would love to have heard that conversation.

*I walked the SWCP to Treyarnon*
*There are a lot of beautiful beaches along the way to gaze upon*
*Even on a dark grey overcast day*
*The golden sands were shining out from every bay*
*At the YHA I had to share a room with smelly Don*

ACCOMODATION – TREYARNON – YHA Best YHA I stayed at.

Day 16

May 16$^{th}$ 2017

Treyarnon to Newquay – 12.6mi [22.05]-my estimate

*Today's songs going through my head went from" Stormy Weather" to Turning Japanese" to "A Hard Rains Gonna Fall" and finishing with" Things Can Only Get Better". It was a very wild, windy and wet night. Mercifully, it wasn't raining when leaving the newly refurbished and very comfortable YHA but was still exceptionally gusty. That made for a rough sea and some huge waves repeatedly crashing into this amazingly rugged stretch of coastline. I took a lot of pics and I really hope they do some justice to what I was witnessing. I took that many I've now got a blister on my index finger tip. The path to Porthcothan mainly follows this coastline and the wow factor was off the scale and easily going up to wowee and above. I've seen some incredible shorelines on this walk to date but today the weather just brought it all to life. I felt very privileged and lucky to be so close to it all. From Porthcothan onwards the rain started, this time sweeping in off the land making walking very uncomfortable, with the wind taking you sideways. The tide was in at the start of the day and a lot of the smaller beaches were hard to see including unfortunately Bedruthan Steps. A stop at the National Trust Cafe near there provided some much needed respite from the elements. On from there and around Trenance Point was a challenge until you then you catch sight of Mawgan Porth. What a picture! There was just wave after wave crashing into the most incredible stretch of golden sands. The tide was receding now and the beach looked huge. Astonishingly, there were two intrepid surfers out there. Blimey O'Reilly those guys had balls. The rain had been intermittent all day but it was dry going around Beryls Point and soon into view is the majestic Watergate Bay. It was low tide and it was stretching out all the way to Newquay. A path over the top of the cliffs takes you almost all the way into the town via the beaches at Porth and Lusty Glaze. A really remarkably stretch of the path and made all the more remarkable by the inclement weather. Wouldn't have minded a bit of sunshine though!*

This was the day the ocean came alive and showed its wilder side for the first time since I started walking. It was driven on by a strong wind that was whipping the sea up into a real frenzy. There's no doubt it can be windier and rougher but today was just about right. It was safe enough to get close to the cliff edges to get some great pics without being too badly buffeted about or risk getting blown over them. There were some more great beaches along the way and Newquay has got a few of its own. I'm not that enamoured with the town centre but you don't have to go far to get escape from it. I introduced Lynn to the delights of Wetherspoons for the first time in the evening; she was mightily impressed. Despite a few beers in there I hardly slept a wink that night as I was staying in a terrible B&B. The place was practically held together with string and sticky tape and little worked including the Wi-Fi. Dodgy wiring, broken locks, loose sinks and generally grubby, it was dire. I looked at some trip advisor reviews and wish I'd done that prior to booking. There was some good feedback from stag parties but most of the others were quite scathing. As always I just tried to put it down to experience and suffered it for the one night. Sometimes you really do get what you pay for and it was very cheap. I didn't hang around for breakfast, which I wasn't prepared to risk.

*I walked the SWCP to Newquay*
*On a windy day there was a wild and rough sea*
*Mawgan Porth has the most magnificent beach*
*The tide recedes so much it almost looks out of reach*
*Today the North Cornwall coast was an awesome place to be*

ACCOMODATION – NEWQUAY - KIRRIBILLI HOTEL B&B Cheap but not cheerful. Pass, literally.

Day 17

May 17th 2017

Newquay to Perranporth – 10.9mi [17.5km]

*Today's song titles started from "Dirty Old Town" to I Gotta Get Out Of This Place" to" Don't Pay The Ferryman" to "Wade In The Water" and finished with "Here Comes The Sun". It was a grey and gloomy morning in Newquay Town which rather matched my mood. Had a sleepless night in the worst B&B I've stayed in so far. The path restarts at the harbour and on walking out to Fistral Beach, I was trying to be positive and think about all of the good things I liked about Newquay. It wasn't easy. Well to start with there were the beaches, then there was the um....beaches and finally the hmm...beaches. At Fistral beach the surfers were in full swing on some good waves. Not quite as spectacular as yesterday's high rollers but still quite wild. Walk around Pentire Point and you arrive at the Gannel Estuary, which you have to cross to continue. The SWCP Association guide book offers four options. Option 1 is the Fern Pit Ferry crossing which was the preferred option owing to tide times. Had been assured by a local that the Ferry had restarted its summer service...wrong! I was reliably informed by the local postie "Ferry crossing don't start till Saturday". I really wish I could convey how it was said in true Cornish Jethro "Train don't*

*stop at Camborne Wednesday" style. Ok, so on to Option 2 further upstream at the Penpole Footbridge Crossing. The problem here was that it was still two foot under water and again reliably informed it would be a good hour before you could walk over. Ok, so on to Option 3 which involved an extra three mile walk which would take way over an hour. Option 4 was totally out of the question as it was even further and would take even longer. So, it wasn't looking good.*
*Then I thought, hang on a jiffy, what about Option 5?*
*"Option 5?" I hear you say,*
*"Yes, Option 5" says I,*
*"There is no Option 5" say you,*
*"Yes there is, I've just thought it through"*
*"Off with your boots, off with your socks,*
*"Roll up your trousers and over the bridge you trots!"*
*Never mind splinters, cuts or falling in, just bloody do it I thought. So I did. No cuts, splinters or soakings, just two very cold feet. Voila, Option 5. Put it in the book! After that it was all very uneventful but still enjoyable. Past Crantock Beach which is my personal Newquay favourite, then on to Polly Joke, around to Holywell Bay and then finishing off by walking along the prodigious Perran beach. The sun had come out by now and my feet had warmed up. It was a lovely end to the day.*

This was a fun day with a gloriously sunny end. I was pleased to get out of Newquay town centre and moving away to areas I was not so familiar with. Crossing the Gannel was a giggle and saved us about an hour of wasted time just sitting around. We set a trend as just before we crossed, two American walkers arrived on our side and were wondering what to do, as were a couple on the other side. There were all hanging around waiting for something to happen and so we went over and they swiftly followed. Perran beach is magnificent and about two miles long. The official path takes you over and through the dunes but if the tide is out, get down on the beach if you can. The dunes path is very difficult to follow and heavy going. We started off going that way but eventually found a way down to the beach. We were staying at the YHA which isn't quite as smart as Treyarnon, but has a great location up a hill overlooking the sands and right on the coast path. When it opened at 5 o'clock we went to reception which was next to the kitchen where there was a delicious smell of cooking emanating. After I'd showered and was sitting in the lounge a lovely old lady in her 80s got a pie out of the oven along with some vegetables. In the meantime an elderly gentleman, presumably her husband was setting up a table for two in the lounge. As well as knives and forks this included wine glasses and a bottle of red. How bloody civilised and make yourself at home was that! I was quite in awe of them. It did however confirm to me that these places really should be renamed. I was thinking along the lines of "long in the tooth" hostel association. Smelly Don was back and this time the dormitory was full with him and four others. I really could have done with a good night's sleep after virtually nil in Newquay last night but it wasn't looking promising. Me and Lyn went down the local "spoons" and returned in the early evening. Bill and Elsie, the elderly couple, had now finished their meal and were in pyjamas and nightdress and preparing to retire for the evening. It was very sweet and touching but still seemed a little odd to me. I did have a massive stroke of luck later that night. For some unknown reason the duty manager offered Lyn a room to herself if she wanted it. Aware of my sleepless night in Newquay she very generously offered it on to me. I could have given them both a big kiss but refrained.

*I walked the SWCP to Perranporth*
*Cornwall has the amazing beaches on display up here in the North*
*I had to cross a river on foot and the water was very cold*
*But to save time I had to do something bold*
*I would hope not to have to do that too often henceforth*

ACCOMODATION – PERRANPORTH - YHA Great location overlooking the beach and right on the coast path.

Day 18

May 18TH 2017

Perranporth to Portreath – 12.2mi [19.7km]

*Song titles today ranged from "Good Day Sunshine" to "Come Fly With Me" to "I Can See For Miles". I woke to a sunny morning at the YHA in Perranporth. The coast path actually goes right by the hostel and straightaway you are on a steady climb. The last two days have been quite cushy on the old pins but today was definitely more demanding and included a right couple of leg wobblers. The path climbs steadily to cliffs out to Cligga Head and hugs the coastline giving great views out to sea and back to Perranporth. This is an area of old mines and quarries which figure quite regularly on this stretch. Then you pass so close to the flight path of the Perranporth Aerodrome that you instinctively duck when a plane goes over. Thereafter is a steep descent to Trevellas Porth and an even steeper ascent, especially if you go over the bridge by the beach and up the wrong path opposite. I sort of thought this was wrong when the walking turned to rock climbing! The guide book tells you to go upstream to cross at the road bridge. I really must start reading the book before I start walking. Back up to the cliffs and almost immediately back down to Trevaunance Cove. This place is a little hidden treasure I think. Lovely little beach, nice looking pub and a few shops. Definitely on the "must go back again" list. You leave here with a sharp climb again and a long walk out along the cliff top to go around St Agnes Head. Then there is a reasonably flat walk to Chapel Porth passing an impressive looking old engine house at Towanroath on the way. The walk out to St Agnes Head is a little dull. It improves once you turn the corner and the characteristic archetypal rugged Cornish Coastline is very much in evidence. This continues pretty much for the rest of the walk. Nice National Trust café at Chapel Porth offers drinks and huge chunks of chocolate cake which you need to help you get up the other side. Once at the top you move on to Porthtowan and another gorgeous golden beach. There really is an absolute plethora of these beaches on this length since before Padstow and I know there's more to come. Really looking forward to seeing what South Cornwall has to offer in the way of comparison. Then onto Portreath with another two testing deep and steeps to overcome along the way. They were both challenging but not cardiac arresting.*

Today was yet another super day walking under blue skies. We also had the first sighting of a relic of Cornwall's illustrious mining heritage with the engine house at Towanroath. It was to be much more prevalent further on down the coast but this was an enticing introduction to what was to come later. I was very impressed with Trevaunance Cove [see picture] which is small but beautifully formed and hidden away. There's just enough there in the way of facilities to provide all you need but not enough to turn it into just another tourist trap. It struck me as the kind of place to sneak away to for a few days and chill out. I understand St Agnes which is slightly inland is also well worth a visit. Portreath is nice enough but as a former industrial harbour town it is a little plain.

*I walked the SWCP to Portreath*
*The path goes around Trevaunance Cove with a beach beneath*
*Chapel Porth is another cove well worth a stop*
*Just beware it's a long climb from there back up to the cliff top*
*The engine house at Towanroath was built to keep the water out from underneath*

ACCOMODATION – PORTREATH - AIR B&B Very central and almost next to a pub which has a restaurant. It had a lovely host who will also do some washing for you.

Day 19

May 19th 2017

Portreath to Hayle – 12.4mi [19.9km]

*Today's songs buzzing around in my head started with "Mr Blue Sky" to "Jimmy Mack" and onto "Circles In The Sand". Lovely morning in Portreath only spoilt by the realisation that somehow I've lost my [almost] waterproof jacket or had it pinched. My only back up was a three quarter length Pac a Mac until I could purchase another one. I was hoping for a dry day. The path to Hayle out of Portreath starts with two testing valley crossings. Then it's quite flat walking above the top of the cliffs with only occasional glimpses of the coast line. After the almost perpetual visual treats of the last two days it all seemed rather dull. Things liven up again though when you get to the extremely foreboding and satanically named Hell's Mouth. This large inlet has a very steep and sheer cliff face which goes a long way down. I don't know why it's called Hell's Mouth but if you ever got stuck down there, you would have a devil of a job getting back up. Then you have to cross a field and on to Navax Point and then Godrevy Point. The Godrevy lighthouse is a major focal point of the whole walk as it can be seen along nearly this whole stretch. Its white structure standing on a rock just out at sea is very striking. On the walk out to the point you pass through a NT run area which includes Kynance and Mutton Cove. Look closely down and you can see a seal, then two and then you realise there's a whole colony down there. There is lots of signage around this area requesting that you talk in whispers and are generally quiet as loud noises upset and frighten the seals. Lord only knows then what the poor little fellows made of the racket when three low flying helicopters flew over. On then and around the Point and the magnificent sight of three miles of sand that stretches out in front of you. It was low tide which allows you to walk nearly all of this along the beach, thereby avoiding a no doubt extremely arduous walk in the dunes above the beach. I thus arrived in Hayle feeling hale and hearty, looking for ale and ready to party! Oh, if only that were true.*

Not the most exciting of walks compared to previous days but I had been spoilt. I'd never been to Hayle previously and wasn't sure what to make of it. The beach without question was superb but was a little underwhelmed by what else was there. The compact town centre was pleasant enough with a variety of cafes and restaurants. I had a decent pub near my B&B which also served good food and I met Lyn there for an evening meal. Showers had been forecast for tomorrow so I thought I'd try on my Pac a Mac just in case it was needed. This had been kindly given to me by Tonia's mum when I stayed with her in Wadebridge. I wasn't expecting to need it but after losing my jacket it might be called into action. It was not a good look and "flasher" was my immediate thought when I saw it on me in the mirror. Lyn found this all highly amusing when I told her later in the pub. Afterwards, for the first time, I met up with another member of the Facebook group. Rick was a Cornishman and had just returned from living in Australia for a number of years. We enjoyed a couple of pints and a chat together. He was very knowledgeable on all things Cornish and the SWCP in general having walked nearly all of it.

*I walked the SWCP to Hayle*
*Hells Mouth would be a great cliff down which to abseil*
*Godrevy Lighthouse can be seen for miles around*
*When you walk near the seals at Kynance Cove try not to make a sound*
*They might just decide to swim away should you fail*

ACCOMODATION – HAYLE - MADHATTERS B&B A good little B&B run by a very entertaining lady called Pauline.

Day 20

May 20th 2017

Hayle to St Ives – 5.6mi [9.0km]

*Just one theme song today" With a Little Help From My Friends". Two of nicest people you could ever wish to meet, a smashing couple called Andy and Jackie drove all the way down from Bristol to walk with me today. Not only that, they also brought me a waterproof jacket to replace the one that went AWOL the other day. Jackie had also made some very tasty homemade cakes. They were with their good friend, another Andy. So we set off from Hayle in good spirits despite the weather looking a little iffy. Unfortunately, today's walk as well as being one of the shortest, was also one of the dullest, especially the first part. It seemed to take forever to get out of the town and involved a fair bit of road walking, traipsing through housing estates and trundling through sand dunes. However, once all the boring bits were out of the way, things did improve and the sun came out. It was also another day of just being astounded by the quality of beaches this county has to offer, Porthkidney Beach was the first gem. The tide was out and this long stretch of sand was looking amazing, it's just a shame about the name. I think they ought to change it to something more glamorous sounding like Waikiki or maybe Bondi? It could do wonders for their tourist trade. You continue from there and walk a path just away from the coastline which involves admiring some wonderful properties overlooking the sea. This takes you to a steep hill going down to the first of the St Ives beaches at Carbis Bay. It's a bit smaller than some but no less attractive and has a smart restaurant. Moving on from there, follow a slight diversion through the grounds of a hotel, down a private road and you're at Porthminster Beach, yet another stunner. In the guide book, today's walk actually finishes here. We carried on walking into sweet little St Ives although it seems to have grown up and out a lot since I was last here about 20 years ago. It is an endearing old fishing village but was predictably rather crowded, it being a Saturday afternoon. However, for some reason it doesn't detract from its appeal like it has done for me in some other touristy places I've been to recently. We then had some lunch in a very nice restaurant overlooking the harbour. A rather short but ultimately enjoyable walk made even better by sharing it with some great company.*

I was very pleased to see Andy and Jackie and not just for the company. Andy very kindly gave me an old walking jacket of his so the flasher mac could go back in the rucksack at least for now. Not the greatest walk although still pleasant enough once you're out of Hayle but that takes a while and isn't pretty. My friends though were more than happy and quite impressed which just served to remind me that I had been spoilt by my previous walks. It is also the shortest walk in the guide book at just 5.6 miles and a predicted time of 2.5 hours. It took us longer than that as we were taking it leisurely and had a stop at Carbis Bay for refreshments. It was nice to have a short easy day and St Ives is as good a place as any to spend a little down time. I still felt that I wanted to walk on further but after St Ives it's not easy as there is nowhere to stay for a long while, so that probably wasn't feasible.

*I walked the SWCP to St Ives*
*It's a captivating place for people to spend their lives*
*With a pleasing vista from the harbour out to sea*
*Lots of people enjoying fish and chips or maybe a cream tea*
*Boys and girls and husbands with their wives*

ACCOMODATION - ST IVES - TAMARISK B&B Very good, little bit of a walk up a hill to get to it but large room and a lounge to yourself.

Day 21

May 21st 2017

St Ives to Pendeen – 13.9mi [22.3km]

*Today's song titles were "Rocky Mountain Way" and "The Long And Winding Road". Well after a couple of easy sobering day's walking it was back on the hard stuff. This stretch is a real potent cocktail of rough and rocky, boggy and bumpy, uppy and downy and twisting and turning. This is pretty much right from the off after leaving St Ives from Porthmeor Beach. I didn't enjoy the first part of this walk at all, struggling over very tough terrain and large boggy patches. It was also poorly signposted which meant I did some unnecessary mileage clambering around two headlands with uninspiring coastline. Things got better near Carn Naun Point as the scenery definitely improved and the sun came out to play. Unfortunately the underfoot conditions got worse. This is a walk where you constantly have to look where you're treading. You were either on stones, or rocks, or boulders, or in muddy bogs or crossing small streams. Your concentration needed to be at an absolute premium as it is proper ankle twisting territory. There were though some real eye catching points especially around Zennor Head and Gurnards Head with the occasional lovely bay and coves. There were a lot of walkers out today, especially females. More than I've seen on any other stretch. This walk never really gives you much time for the feet to have a breather as there's very little flat grassy land. It's also constantly curving and winding its way around and up and down large headlands. There's no real big up and downers but just constantly walking on rocks in the path or climbing over large boulders. This also made it difficult at times to see where the path was going as it just got lost in the terrain. I did manage to get my head up to notice some seals at one point and River Cove was mightily impressive. Towards the end of the path I walked a short distance with seven young ladies from Kent. They had never done any distance walking previously but yesterday they walked from Perranporth to Hayle which by my reckoning was about 25 miles. Today they were going from Hayle to Lands End which by their reckoning was about 28 miles! I was with them walking around the back of a smashing little beach called Portheras Cove and then waved them on their way approaching Pendeen Watch lighthouse. I was quite pleased the walk was over and definitely pleased I wasn't going to Lands End. This was one to endure rather than enjoy.*

Lyn missed out on this walk and for her that was probably the right decision. I really didn't enjoy it. Judging by the reaction to this post on the Facebook group I wasn't the only one but there were also many others that did. It was hard work but not in the physically exhausting up and down way that I'd experienced previously. It was just so very awkward to walk on with having to constantly watch every step you took for fear of serious injury. I found this mentally very tiring and it detracted from the undoubted raw unspoilt beauty of this stretch. It was also one of the more poorly signposted parts of the coast path. You basically had to determine your own way through the terrain which just added to the effort needed to get you through what was a very difficult section.

*I walked the SWCP to Pendeen*
*It was tough and rough and mean*
*The path was winding and long*
*It seemed to go on and on*
*I won't walk it again but I'm glad I've been*

ACCOMODATION – PENDEEN - THE OLD CHAPEL B&B Superb modernisation of an old building. It's all open plan and very impressive. There is a very likable and friendly couple who own it.

# WEEK FOUR

Day 22

May 22nd 2017

Pendeen to Sennen Cove – 9.3mi [14.9km]

*Today's theme songs were "Going Underground"," Fly Me To The Moon" and finished with "Walking On Sunshine". It was a new day, a new stretch of path and a new landscape to marvel at. Bit of a grey gloomy start to the day in Pendeen but the forecast was promising. The overcast skies seemed to be quite fitting when I arrived at the old mining area of Geevor which was eerily quiet. Just a little further on the path though the sun was coming through at the Levant Mine. This was the start of a length of path with the most amazing iconic Cornish mining heritage scenery. Although a lot of the old buildings are slowly crumbling away, some are still in great condition and they all just seemed to blend in with the surroundings so perfectly. It was quite something and real Poldark country. I almost thought I could hear Demelza's voice shouting out "Ross! Ross! For goodness sake put your shirt back on!" The whole section of path from Botallack to Cape Cornwall is just a joy to walk. The view in the distance of the chimney pointing up to the sky from the top of the mound on Cape Cornwall is quite a sight. Never mind Cape Cornwall it put me in mind of the Apollo moon mission lift offs from Cape Canaveral back in the day. A walk to the top is rewarded with terrific views back inland and along the coastline. From there the path gets a little tougher as you head up towards and then down to a cove at Porth Naven. Climbing up from there and further on and you do hit a rocky path similar to yesterday but not as extreme. It does get tougher though and like yesterday it's sometimes difficult to see the path ahead and you do have to choose between a rock and a hard place at times. This section though is much better signposted with a lot of granite waymarks. Much of the rest of the walk is like this but all the time along high cliff tops with great views. You also walk through a NT conservation area for the Cornish Chough but alas the little fellas were being very shy. Would have been well chuffed to have seen one. On to Gwynver beach where the tide was in and the waves stirring up a good head of surf. On a little further and you're soon at Sennen Cove which is another great beach for the surfing dudes amongst you. It was a wonderful walk on a glorious day.*

This was a very varied and interesting section. I was up and about quite early to walk back down to where I had finished off yesterday. Met up with Lyn once I got to Levant as she was back walking again today, she had stayed further down the path the previous night. It was good to have her company again. Walking from there to Botallack was an easy and relatively flat walk, with a lot of mining relics to stop and admire along with the imposing engine houses. Then it gets more strenuous as you steadily advance towards the majestic headland of Cape Cornwall with its protruding chimney the dominant focal point. We stopped for a break as there is a neat little mobile café close to the car park nearby. After that point the coastline reverts back to rugged and rocky with small isolated coves and some bigger beaches. We passed two great beaches at Gwynver and at our final destination of Sennen Cove. Both have long stretches of golden sand and are popular with surfers due to the Atlantic swell. There is also a cracking pub at Sennen Cove called The Old Success Inn and this is where we had our habitual beer and crisps.

*I walked the SWCP to Sennen Cove*
*It was a great path to walk but many have drove*
*The landscape was utterly beguiling*
*With many reminders of the old days of mining*
*And then on to Sennen I strove*

ACCOMMODATION – SENNEN - SUNNYBANK HOUSE About a mile out of the Cove up a hill, reasonably priced and spotlessly clean.

Day 23

May 23rd 2017

Sennen Cove to Newlyn – 16mi [25.6km]-my estimate

*Today's songs were" Fog On The Tyne", "I Can't Stand Up For Falling Down" and finished with "I Can See Clearly Now". All ready for a long walk today. I was up with the chough and about to be full of breakfast baked beans. Jumped out of bed, pulled down the blinds and ...WHAT THE FFFFOG! I was supposed to be at Lands End soon. I couldn't see any land never mind the end! I thought it might be condensation and started frantically rubbing the window pane but it was still there. I then went downstairs for breakfast and learnt about last night's really genuine bad news. That put my piffling, piddling pathetic problems into perspective. So off I went to find Lands End, I knew it was out there somewhere. Set off from Sennen harbour following the coast path although there were a whole myriad of little paths going on. Got to Lands End or at least I presumed it was. I found the pub and the sign anyway. Someone had told me you could see the Scilly Isles from there. On a morning like this, that wasn't just silly, it was plain ridiculous. I continued on in the murk catching occasional glimpses of coastline. I could see it, I could hear it, I could almost touch it, I just couldn't ruddy see it. Things did improve slightly by Porthgwarra. The path was quite even and gentle but there was the odd patch of rocky terrain. When I reached Porthcurno things got even better. I love this area, especially The Minack Theatre which is a marvellous mystical arena. I was lucky enough to see a performance on a lovely summers evening here last year. It was "The Merry Wives of Windsor" by some bloke called Shake Speare. Well Shakey, I think Shakin Stevens could have done better. He needs to throw more gags in if he's going to have any future writing comedies. No one was laughing and it got even worse when a sea fret came in and you couldn't see a thing! He ought to write some serious stuff. But it didn't matter a jot, it was an amazing experience. You leave here from the back of the beach, up a steepish path to Percella Point and then a long flattish walk above the cliffs. You descend to Penberth Cove, a tiny fishing hamlet, before the next really tough clamber at Porthguarnon. A big descent and a massive climb back up those giant wooden steps. It was harder than any climb I'd done in a while but from there it's a level walk through some woods and down to St Loy. You then have a tricky clamber along a big boulder beach, back up behind a lighthouse and then the descent to Lamorna. The last part into the Cove is a really testing walk/climb over some massive rocks. I slipped twice and went completely A over T. The first time I was lucky and had a softish landing but still grazed my knees and got bad nettle stings, it might have been much worse. Lamorna Cove sounds lovely but is something and nothing and I was a little disappointed. If you need to use the toilet here I have a top tip for you. Don't bother looking for signs on doors saying Gents and Ladies or looking for those figures they put on toilet doors these days. Those ones where it takes you five minutes to work out if it's male or female and you still get it wrong! No, all you have to do is look for the door with wait for it ...the number 2 on it! I shit you not! Never saw a number 1 door anywhere. On then to Mousehole along a tricky track which was extremely boggy in places. I like Mousehole; it's very cute and Cornish, just a shame about the silly name. A little further on is Newlyn and my walking day was over. It was long but I enjoyed it. I just wish I'd seen more of it!*

Today got off to a bad start with the weather playing up. It was the only time on my whole trip that I had to deal with thick fog and it's really frustrating. I was here for all the amazing scenery and up to date it had massively exceeded my expectations. Yet here I was at probably the most iconic and famous place on the path and could see virtually nothing. The path was also difficult to follow in places and in the guide book it made a couple of references to alternative scenic paths. Normally I would have been very keen to follow these but today it would have been a pointless exercise. At least it did start to clear around lunchtime but by then Lands End was long gone and I never walked backwards. This was another occasion when with a more flexible schedule it may have possible to have returned another day to see what I had missed. Lyn and I parted ways at The Minack Theatre, she wanted to do the tour and was getting public transport from there to Lamorna where she had booked her B&B. I was staying a fair distance past Lamorna which was the day's recommended stopping point. This was purely due to me being unable to get any reasonably priced accommodation in the area. I was going on to Newlyn which made for a long day but a very short one tomorrow. I enjoyed my afternoon solo walk as although quite strenuous, I could at least see some splendid views when the fog lifted. When I got to Lamorna Cove I was pleased to not be staying there as it was plain and uninspiring. Mousehole on the other hand is delightful and I would have liked to have stayed there but again the tourist inflated accommodation prices meant I decided against it. My Air B&B in Newlyn was great and the hosts very friendly but the pub I went to along the road for a meal less so. As soon as you entered, it felt like the locals closed ranks and turned their backs towards you at the bar. I wasn't overly concerned. I had my pint and some fish and chips and was soon gone.

*I walked the SWCP to Newlyn*
*It was a long walk and very foggy to begin*
*At Porthgwarra and Porthcurno it slowly got clearer*
*On past Lamorna and Mousehole I got nearer and nearer*
*I was tired when I finished, tomorrow I might have a lie in*

ACCOMODATION – NEWLYN - AIR B&B Nice house and room, very clean and comfortable. Good location right on the coast path between Mousehole and Penzance.

Day 24

May 24th 2017

Newlyn To Marazion – 5.5mi [13km]-my estimate

*Today's songs going through my head were" Give A Little Whistle", "The Tide Is High" and "Sitting On The Dock Of The Bay". Woke up and gingerly looked out the window with a little trepidation after yesterday. Hooray! No fog, no mist, no rain, sleet or snow. No worries. A little overcast but a forecast of sun later. Well, in distance terms, if yesterday's walk was a marathon, than todays was a sprint. It was a walkover, literally, around the bay to Marazion and St Michaels Mount. Set off from Newlyn and passed the harbour onto a long promenade into Penzance. Well I didn't see any pirates along the way but I did bump into Mr Henk van Leersum aka "The Walking Dutchman" and a regular contributor on the group. Henk was on his way to Porthcurno but was walking wounded. The poor chap had a very nasty blister/cut on his foot. I advised caution as Porthcurno is a tough walk with two good feet. I carried on my way onto the extremely flat cycle path almost all the way into Marazion. As the tide was out I did walk over the sand until I got to a little river. Tried jumping over and failed miserably. There is a bridge for the more sensible. On then to the causeway and out to the Mount. You cannot help but be massively impressed by this place. How the devil did they ever build it all those years ago? Got to give credit to those monks, in between all that silence and praying they didn't mind getting their hands dirty. I wonder how that silent thing worked if they dropped a massive stone on their foot or hammered a nail through a finger. Didn't go up to the castle as I have been there fairly recently but well worth the time and money if you haven't. Back on the mainland the town was very busy but still quite quaint and charming. About lunchtime the tide came in, the causeway was covered, the sun came out and it was scorchio time; really hot. In true Ross Poldark style the shirt came off for the first time. I was even contemplating a swim but only had my Pac a Mac to change under. On a busy beach with many children around not only would that have looked very wrong, it could also have gone very wrong! I refrained and will save a swim for another day. Hope to have more interesting and informative things to post tomorrow. I'm off now to get a big towel.*

This was probably the shortest day of the whole walk and also very flat. It was another instance where with slightly better preparation I may have done it differently. At the early planning stage I did think it would be nice to have the occasional short day. I hadn't planned any specific rest days so short days were the next best thing. It was also good to meet Henk who was the second person I'd met from the group after Rick in Hayle. I was somewhat surprised when I heard a voice shouting out in a Dutch accent "Hey John, it's Henk, I follow you on Facebook" but I did instantly recognise him and he was very friendly. He was very anxious to show me the pictures he had taken of his injured bloodied foot on his phone. What he wasn't to know was I'm quite squeamish about stuff like that. I've seen many episodes of Casualty but not all the way through. As soon as it gets gory, I get going, usually to the kitchen to make a cuppa. From what I did see through my fingers it looked in a bad way and I was amazed when he later posted that he had made it to Lands End. I thought he'd do well to make it to a hospital. I started referring to him as "The Crazy Dutchman" after that. Seriously, he is a smashing chap and loves the SWCP with a passion. He also later posted some great pics from Lands End to show me what I had missed yesterday due to the fog fiasco. Cheers Henk, it looked amazing and I confess to being just a tad gutted. Once I got to Marazion I joined the throng walking out along the causeway to St Michaels Mount. Lyn met me later over there and she did the whole SMM tour including the gardens. I went back to the mainland and had a late lunch in the Cutty Sark. It was that good I went back in the evening with Lyn for dinner. She was having some foot problems herself now and restricted her walking to allow time for some healing.

*I walked the SWCP to Marazion*
*The forecast was good, one I hoped to rely on*
*The walk wasn't far*
*About fifteen minutes by car*
*But this isn't a path to cheat on*

ACCOMODATION – MARAZION - CHYVELLAN COTTAGE B&B Delightful property, a short walk uphill just on the outskirts of Marazion with a huge garden.

Day 25

May 25th 2017

Marazion to Porthleven – 10.6mi [17.1km]

*Just one song title today which was "Lovely Day". I jumped out of bed to be greeted by an absolutely glorious morning. I was staying in a B&B just outside Marazion in a quaint old country cottage, with a garden akin to a mini country estate. It's owned and run by a smashing older couple. Another chap called Joe and his partner were also staying, we had met briefly yesterday evening. At breakfast Joe was asking me about my walking. So I asked him what had brought him here. It was early and I was still half asleep but I could have sworn he said "I like ghouls". This took me a bit by surprise but ghost hunting is quite popular I believe these days. So I replied "Oh right, you're looking for spirits". He shook his head and repeated slowly this time "lichen and galls"! Cue very blank expression on my face. I kind of had a rough idea about lichen but galls meant diddly squat to me. I had to confess my ignorance to Joe and I could tell he looked very disappointed in me. Then followed a very one sided conversation with him waxing lyrical about galls especially and me expressing the occasional "ok", and "is that right" and "oh really". I've never eaten a full English breakfast so quick in my life. Apologies to all you lichen and galls lovers out there. I like to be out and about and surrounded by nature but I'm very much a townie when it comes to knowing much about it. Off I went then on my merry way through the main road out of Marazion, a path takes you down to and across a beach. All the while you are close to the bay with St Michaels Mount dominating the seascape but as the bay curves around you see a little different side to it as you go. The walk so far is level and easy going. You soon arrive at another little known gem called Perranuthnoe which is a fetching little beach with parking and refreshments. On then to Cudden Point with a bit of a leg stretcher getting up there but still with a great view all the around the bay and back to SMM. A lot of the walk thus far has been on low cliffs and fields. On from there and SMM is now out of view but it's a lovely walk around a succession of small coves. After here you reach Kenneggy Sands, a beautiful long stretch of sandy beach. It's only accessible at low tide with a walk over some boulders from Prussia Cove. Not far on from there is Praa Sands. It's longer than Kenneggy and easily accessible with a car park, toilets and shops. It's also very nice but I know which one of the two I'd prefer. After leaving Praa Sands via some sand dunes the walk changes complexion and gradually gets a little tougher. The sun and warmth accentuate the beauty before you but it also places more emphasis on the effort you have to put in. However, it was no less enjoyable. Up and over Rinsey Head and you're walking past another one of the iconic restored engine house that were so prevalent a few days ago. On around Trewavas Head and there's some more. From that point you can see Porthleven in the distance but you can also see high cliffs and steps leading up to them. This is where you really earn your post walk beers. The steps do take your breath away but you're soon into Porthleven. This place took me by surprise. It's superb with an attractive little harbour, shops and restaurants around it and a fabulous beach. It's got all the appeal of Padstow and St Ives but without the tourists. A real find, I thoroughly enjoyed my walk today.*

I walked this section alone as Lyn was still having problems. She caught the bus and met me in Porthleven when I had finished. She missed a good one. The day begun on an odd note at breakfast as described above. Joe and his missus were a bit of a peculiar couple. He was a biggish chap, middle aged, with a long grey beard and dressed in checked shirt, braces and three quarter length trousers. His wife was a diminutive, nervous lady who seemed keen to impress Joe but he very quickly corrected her if she got anything wrong. This made me feel a little awkward. They described their two day break as an experiment. They didn't elaborate and I didn't pursue the matter but had the distinct impression though that Mrs

Joe didn't get out much. It was a smashing day and the walk itself was an absolute peach. It was easy to start with at least and all the while staying close to the coast with wonderful views. There were more outstanding beaches along the way including some discreet ones as well as the popular and well known. As you can tell I really liked Porthleven, probably because I'd never heard of it previously and wasn't expecting much. We had a couple of beers after the walk in the Ship Inn which went down very well. In the evening we had a meal outside on the quay at the Harbour Inn which I would thoroughly recommend.

*I walked the SWCP to Porthleven*
*I was very keen to go and was up at seven*
*The day was sunny and hot*
*Boring it was definitely not*
*It was a lovely little stretch of heaven*

ACCOMODATION – PORTHLEVEN - AIR B&B Great location just above the harbour, large converted loft room.

Day 26

May 26th 2017

Porthleven to The Lizard – 13.9mi [22.3km]

*I woke up with a tune in my head that hardly left it all day. "I'm off to see the Lizard",*
*"The wonderful Lizard of the SWCP",*
*"Because, because, because, because, because",*
*"Because of the wonderful views that it has"*
*Also, because it's my last day on the path for a while but an absolutely showstopper of a walk to go out on. It was another glorious morning with the sun singing loudly and out on my own yellow brick road. A bit cooler and breezier than yesterday but that was welcome. Left pretty Porthleven and made my way out towards the Loe Bar. I wasn't sure how to pronounce that but I was guessing Loe as in Lou Macari or Lou Rowles or even loo rolls but probably wrong. This is a strip of sand that separates the sea from a creek and you walk straight down the middle like Moses. From here is a lovely walk above cliffs and over more coves and beaches. On then past Gunwalloe Fishing Cove and onto Gunwalloe Church Cove with a quaint little church next to another superb beach. The first half of today's walk is very easy with just a few minor undulations. After here you move on around Poldhu and Polurrian Coves, both were attractive. After Poldhu Cove you turn a sharp right on up to the cliffs and past the Marconi Centre where they make all types of pasta. Keep going and enjoying the great coastline and you end down in Mullion Cove which has a harbour and a very reasonable café. After leaving Mullion the walk gets a little tougher but this next section is up with all the very best I've seen so far on this journey. A nice fairly easy walk follows through the The Lizard National Nature Reserve which is a treat for all you lovers of flora and fauna and birdwatchers. The rugged rock coastline is also very awe inspiring. Then the*

*only really difficult part of the walk is the slippery stony descent into Gew Graze and a steep climb back up to the top of the cliffs. The path then takes you around Rill Point and you suddenly catch sight of Kynance Cove. What a stunning, spectacular spellbinding view that is. Absolutely blew me away. My vocabulary can't express what it looks like in any way to do it justice. Got my old index finger blister back I was taking that many pictures. Large rock formations just emerging from a brilliant turquoise coloured sea with small sandy beaches. A-MA-ZING as Craig whats-his-name from Strictly would say. The WOWometer exploded! Just spent ages walking around above it and then down to the beach. To continue you then cross to the other side and on to Old Lizard Head and finally The Lizard passing still more superb coastline.*
*Well that's it for me until June 5th. It's half time for me and I'm back off to Brizzle for a break. I'm feeling a little jaded and need to reinvigorate myself. I don't want to get WOW fatigue. Also, being away for nearly four weeks I need to cut the grass, feed the cat, sign on and study up on my lichens and galls. Bye for now.*

I was so happy that my last day on the path prior to my break was such a brilliant one. It was another wonderful walk with superb weather. Again unfortunately Lyn was unable to walk which was a real shame as she missed an absolute bobby-dazzler. Nice and reasonably flat with a succession of alluring beaches. I hadn't been for a swim up to this point and did tip my toes in the sea at a few places but still too cold for me. Lyn was getting to be a dab hand with the bus timetables and met me at Mullion Cove which was about half way. We had a superb cream tea with huge scones at Porthmellin café down on the harbour. I then carried on my way but Lyn hung around and later got another bus to The Lizard. For the umpteenth time I was just astonished by the abundance of beauty along this coastline. Then just when I thought I'd seen it all, I set eyes on Kynance Cove and it just stopped me in my tracks. It was pure, raw and simply breathtaking. Lyn met me as I came along the last length of path to The Lizard and we went and had a drink at the café there. It was a super day and a lot of people were enjoying the weather here at the most southerly point of mainland UK. My walking was over now for a week or so. I was happy to be going home after nearly four weeks away but also looking forward to resuming this amazing adventure. I was overwhelmed by the response I had to my last post and a photo saying "bye for now". Most of the replies said thanks and wished me a restful break, with a lot of people expressing their enjoyment of my daily blog and even the limericks. A few members of the group even entered into the spirit of the limerick by sending me some and very good they were. I forgot to do one on the day so here's one to fill that gap.

*I walked the SWCP to The Lizard*
*With scenery so magical, it must have been created by a wizard*
*I stopped along the way for a delicious cream tea*
*The weather was so good I almost went for a dip in the sea*
*I definitely wouldn't have done that if I'd walked here in a blizzard*

ACCOMODATION - THE LIZARD – YHA Superb location and in a great building which was once a Victorian hotel.

I had a terrible night's sleep in the YHA. These are just not good places for light sleepers. I was sharing a dorm with two chaps. One guy was either at death's door or a massive hypochondriac. When I arrived he had already been there a while and had filled two large shelves with a vast array of pills, potions, medicines and vitamins. He was a one man walking pharmacy. Just a shame for me he couldn't do anything about his propensity for flatulence which was persistent through the night. The other dorm guest was just a nonstop thundering snoring machine which shook the room. I never really saw him as he was already in bed with his snores reverberating around the room when I retired about 10.30. Then just as I finally got to sleep, he was up, dressed and gone at five in the morning. Also, the YHA is right next to the lighthouse and at some point in the night the foghorn started with its persistent deep mournful hum. That wasn't ever going to help my insomnia. Lyn and I left quite early in the morning. We went up to the village to try and get some breakfast but had to hang around for a while waiting for somewhere to open. We caught the same bus out with me heading for Falmouth to get a train and Lyn heading for Coverack. We both had to change buses at Helston and then go our separate ways. It was a sad moment when we separated especially because Lyn had gone to check out some bus times at another stop further up the road. My bus arrived and I had to get on without saying goodbye; we could only wave frantically at each other as me and the bus went past her. It was a shame as I wanted to say goodbye properly and give her a big hug for being such a great walking companion. We had though made some tentative plans to meet up later on in Devon at some point and keep in touch by e-mail.

I arrived back at The Lizard on the Sunday afternoon with my great mate Pete. We have been friends for many years and although our lives had taken us in completely different directions geographically they were definite parallels. He had taken some time off work and was going to walk with me for three days. The weather for my week away from the path had been very good and our journey down to Cornwall was accompanied by glorious sunshine. However, the weather forecast for the next week was not good and especially the next day when an unseasonal low was moving in. Strong winds and raining cats and dogs and rabbits and any other domestic pet you care to name. Pete though was being eternally optimistic and that definitely kept my spirits up.

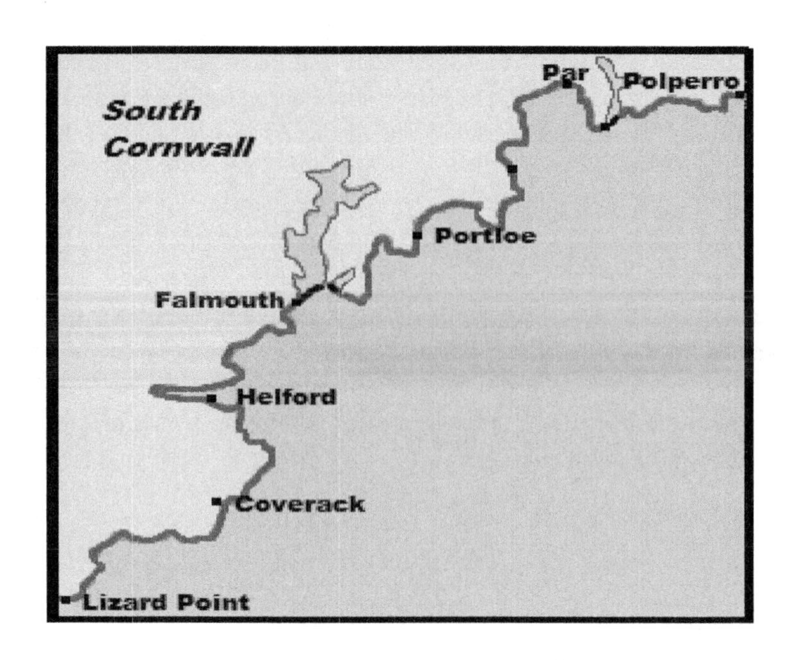


# WEEK FIVE

Day 27

June $5^{th}$ 2017

The Lizard to Coverack – 10.6mi [17.1km]

*Warm sunshine, clear blue sky and a cool gentle breeze are all the meteorological conditions you require for a great days walk on the path. Sadly, all were completely absent from the skyline this morning. Something must have upset The Lizard overnight. Yesterday afternoon when we arrived it was calm, peaceful and beautiful but this morning it was now angry, agitated and ugly. Perhaps someone had been poking it with a big stick. Never mind I was happy to be back after a week or so and I was not alone. My mate of many years Pete was with me and keen to experience some of the magic of the SWCP. He's from the North, a place called Winterfell (aka*

*Sheffield) so he's used to bad weather and was being positive despite the grey scenario and the foreboding skies. So off we trotted in the wind and rain although neither was too bad at this stage. The path was muddy and slippery but not too demanding. We made it to cute little Cadgwith Cove in good time and good shape and continued onto Poltesco and down to Kennack Sands. Not a lot of people around today so the beaches and coves were looking at their naked best despite the inclement weather. It was at this point though that the wind started to get stronger and was whipping the waves into a right old frenzy which I love to see. However, the going was getting much tougher and we were starting to go sideways. But we pressed on and down and up Beagles Point which is the one big river valley crossing on this stretch and definitely no pushover. From here to Black Head the wind really kicked in. We must have looked like a couple of drunks staggering home after being out on a massive bender. We were literally at least four sheets to the wind. We struggled on but progress was slow with the rain getting heavier and now coming at you horizontally. The wind was very persistent and nobody wants persistent wind do they? It was thoroughly miserable but not far to go now and we would be home and dry. We came then to the final leg, Chynhalls Point. This is where you have to decide between the inland path to Coverack and the official lower path to Porthbeer Cove and then into Coverack. Well in for a penny, in for a pound we thought, we'll go down. Well, I would want much more than a pound to do it again under today's brutal conditions. It is seriously walking career threatening terrain. God knows how many people must have injured themselves walking this path. I went down most of it on my arse which I think was probably the safest way today. It reminded me of when I first learnt to ski only much more difficult. Seriously, be very wary of this path. It really should have a health warning. We managed to get through it though miraculously with no injuries and then on to Coverack and the shelter of the Paris Hotel. It was really bloody awful at this point and I was very glad today's walk was over. On reflection it was definitely the worst conditions I've walked in so far but I was proud to have done it and even more proud of Pete. He's not a walker as such and is beset with a few serious health problems. There really couldn't have been a worse day to have completed your first section of this great path and he didn't complain at all. Well done mate. It was memorable.*

We woke to an overcast and drizzly morning which was windy but not too bad. Things deteriorated slowly but surely, culminating in a truly awful last hour or so. There were some sections on this coast path where I was very pleased to not be today. Hartland Quay to Bude and St Ives to Pendeen were just two that sprung immediately to mind. This was bad enough, especially that last extremely slippery treacherous path. It was ridiculously steep, overgrown and full of rocks and stones. Someone will get hurt badly there if they haven't already. I was lucky to have had Pete with me as I would definitely have struggled alone on that walk. It was one of the few days where on my own I may have been questioning my sanity and the worthiness of this whole venture. We did get lucky with our accommodation that evening as it was owned by a smashing couple. They had a big house with a glowing Aga, warming up a large lounge where we and others staying could leave boots, jackets, trousers etc. to dry overnight. They also had the radiators on in the room so if you needed to, you could wash and dry your smaller items. It was just what was needed after that awful day. It was good to have company in the evening and we took a wander along the promenade back to the Paris hotel for food and booze.

*I walked the SWCP to Coverack*
*It was a very wet, muddy and slippery track.*
*I walked it with my mate Pete*
*A nicer chap you couldn't meet*
*Despite the weather it was great to be back*

ACCOMODATION – COVERACK - PENMARTH HOUSE B&B Big house with nice rooms and good breakfast.

Day 28

June 6th 2017

Coverack to Helford – 13.1mi [21.1km]

*The morning sky was blue and full of sunshine. I know it was early doors but the omens were promising. The harbingers of doom had been very vocal the evening before with threats of thunderstorms and bottomless bogs. So off we set with Coverack looking wonderful in the early morning sunshine. Pete was paying the penalty of the previous day's exertions with a foot injury so we weren't rushing. The first obstacle to overcome was a little unexpected. A small herd of cows were blocking our way at a stile so Pete encouraged me to use my "cow whisperer "skills. This amounted to me very slowly climbing the stile and calling moove along please, moove along, like a bus conductor but it seemed to work and we were soon mooveing along ourselves and on our way again. The next small problem was just before Lowland Point which was a little boggy but out came my adjustable stilts and we were up and over in no time. The next stretch up to Porthallow I have to say was probably the most uninspiring and unphotogenic length of path that I have walked for some time. We reached Fat Apples Cafe in good time and still the sun was shining and no sign of thunderstorms. In fact it hadn't rained a drop. Unfortunately, Pete disgraced himself by committing the cardinal faux pas in Cornwall by getting his jam and cream in the wrong order when we were having some lovely warm homemade scones. He was given an instant lifetime ban from Fat Apples and quite rightly so. His only defence was to quote the Yorkshire motto "I like what I bloody well do and I do what I bloody well like". Not good enough especially as although he lives there he's not a genuine Yorkie. Porthallow as many of you are probably aware is the half way point on the SWCP. It's a great feeling to get there although tinged with sadness as it means there will soon be less than half to go and it will be all over. Anyway, on from there and the weather just got better and better as did the coastline. The path itself although a little wet, muddy and overgrown in places was still very level. No hills on this section. On we walked to Nare Point passing some very pretty beaches on the way and further on to the gorgeous Gillan Cove glistening in the sunshine. What a sweet little place this is, real picture postcard stuff with green hills all around and boats bobbing away in the creek. As Pete was struggling a little and the tide was high we called for the ferry and crossed with some other walkers. On then past St Anthony Church and up across a field. Then a long walk into Helford through some woods and past some very cute coves. The sun was still shining out with a strong breeze but no sign of any rain. Helford is a delightful little village and we soon found our way to the Shipwrights Arms. Our accommodation was the extremely impressive Sail Loft and it was right opposite the pub. It was the perfect end to a great day.*

We had a great day's walk and I'm glad Pete got to see the path in a better light than it showed itself yesterday. I believe we may have been luckier today with the weather, as apparently in other parts of the South West the winds were very strong and there was still a lot of rain around. We managed to miss the rain altogether and the wind only got blustery late on near the day's finish. What a great place to finish as well. Helford went straight on the "must go back to" list and I would definitely stay at the Sail Loft again.

*I walked the SWCP to Helford*
*Despite the weather forecast it never rained, it never poured*
*Who would have thought the cure for sore bones*
*Could be found in cream and jam and fresh scones*
*It was a great little walk, one to be adored*

ACCOMODATION – HELFORD - THE SAIL LOFT This was a self-contained loft room in an annexe away from the main house.

Day 29

June 7th 2017

Helford to Falmouth – 10.0mi [16.1km]

*Woke up in the Sail Loft to a beautiful morning, the sun was streaming in and we had a tremendous view across the river. Unfortunately, the day was all a bit downhill far from then and so was the walk, although not literally. First job was to cross the river over to Helford Passage. So we walked down to the jetty and opened up the smiley face signal board and waited. Eventually over came Bryan and his Ferry. By this time there were a few other walkers in groups waiting. He asked if we wanted to keep in our separate groups and cross when he returned but we said "come on, come on let's stick together". We wanted to stay with "the in crowd". The crossing was smooth and we were soon on our way to the other side. However, it was quite evident that Pete was struggling. He had taken on the path with courage and tenacity on Monday in atrocious conditions but at some cost.*

*Yesterday his ankle was playing up and today his knees as well. It was slow progress but he struggled on with me giving him sympathetic encouragement like "hurry up" and "get a move on". It got that bad at one stage that to try and alleviate the pain he was walking downhill backwards. I had to stifle a snigger or two but it wasn't easy. Other walkers were passing us and giving him some very strange looks; I had to pretend he wasn't with me. Never mind walking from Poole to Minehead, this really was "wrong way walking". He struggled on bravely and fortuitously the path was pretty level in most parts. We eventually left the Helford Passage behind and passed on by some small coves and beaches. The coastline was pleasant enough but nothing remarkable. We eventually reached Maenporth and Pete finally gave up the unequal struggle and decided to get a taxi to Falmouth. To be fair, he missed very little on the remaining trek into Falmouth. Swanpool and Gyllyngvase beaches are nice enough but I guess I've been spoilt and seen better. I reached Falmouth after a long road walk via Pendennis Point. Pete's walk with me is now over and his plan was always to only go as far as Falmouth anyway. He's back to Sheffield tomorrow for an ankle, knee and hip replacement and to change his name to Steve Austin. He was going by train but is now thinking of chartering an Air Ambulance. I'm carrying on to Portloe tomorrow with high hopes of a more enjoyable day. I shall miss the old git.*

This was a bit of a drab day really. The weather turned dull after a bright start and so was the walk especially the later stages. Pete was really in quite a bit of pain and progress was slow. It didn't really matter too much as today was a short one but I was relieved as he was when he bailed out at Maenporth. I carried on to Falmouth but not with much enthusiasm. There are occasionally days like these on the path but usually interspersed between other much more interesting ones. I just got on with it in the expectation there would be many better walks ahead. At least it gave me and Pete a chance to have a few beers together as this was his last day. We were staying in a small back street pub just up from the high street. When we left to go into town in the afternoon, the pub was closed. We had a meal and drinks in the centre and then returned quite early not expecting a lot to be going on. Well, when we got back the place was rammed, it was almost standing room only. There was a great atmosphere and it was quiz night, so we had a go and a few more beers. It was a good night for him to bow out on.

*I walked the SWCP to Falmouth*
*I was pleased when it finished I'd had enough*
*I wouldn't describe it as dire*
*But it definitely failed to inspire*
*I'm sure it will be better further along the South*

ACCOMODATION – FALMOUTH - SEAVIEW INN Nice pub and quite popular especially on quiz night. It has clean, comfortable rooms and a decent breakfast.

Day 30

June 8th 2017

Falmouth to Portloe – 13.7mi [22.0km]

*Up early to a grey drizzly morning. After a rather mundane walk yesterday, I was looking forward to a better day. Said goodbye to Pete and despite being battered and bruised he's hooked on the SWCP. He'll be back just as soon as all his joints have been replaced. So off I trotted down to the Prince of Wales Pier to board the first of two ferries needed to get to St Anthony. I arrived just after nine and all was strangely quiet but it was early. A chap walked by and I asked him:*
*"Where do I get the ferry to St Mawes?"*
*"Over there mate"*
*"Thank you"*
*"Tomorrow"*
*"Pardon?"*
*"Tomorrow mate"*
*"Hold up, what happened to today? I haven't been up long, it can't have finished already?"*
*"All today's ferries are cancelled"*
*"What!"*
*"It's too rough out there"*
*"Seriously? It doesn't look that rough"*
*"Well, it is and the ferries aren't running"*
*Obviously I'm not Ben Ainslie but it honestly didn't look rough.*
*Anyway, a complete panic set in and I didn't have a Scooby Doo about what to do next but thankfully a lady at the visitor information did. Catch the bus to Truro and then one to St Mawes or Portscatho. Both were very useful suggestions but also with drawbacks. The walk from St Mawes is too far and takes too long and walking from Portscatho meant I would miss out a small part of the path. This rankled and would have bugged me all the rest of the trip. I was contemplating getting a taxi from Portscatho to St Anthony. However, a*

*very helpful driver on the no 50 bus suggested getting off at Gerrans and walking to Place where the ferry lands. As this is also in the guide book with directions that's what I decided to do, but it did mean extra mileage and another hour on what was going to be an already long day. I rang the Fal river company to check on the chances of the St Mawes crossing in the afternoon and was told slim and nil. So a very hastily prepared plan B went into action. Off the bus at Gerrans church and down a long wet muddy but flat lane. Eventually this led to a path to the woods and a nice scenic ramble along the river to the ferry landing point. Just before I got there and it all looked very calm to me, I could have sworn I saw a small water taxi crossing. I very nearly gave the Fal river company a fal mouthed phone call. So basically I was where I should have been about two hours earlier but at least I was there. The walk itself was an immediate improvement on yesterday. There were great views across the river and a nice green albeit muddy path all the way around St Anthony Head and on to the lighthouse. It had also stopped raining and the sun was coming out to play. On then to Portscatho and it was a well maintained track, which meant I could make up some time but also enjoy the beautiful coastline and beaches like Porthbeor and Towan. This was the SWCP I crave so much. Made it to Portscatho in great time and stopped for a cuppa. The weather was very much betwixt and between all day. Showers and then warm sunshine and back to showers. I was doing more clothing changes than a model during a one woman catwalk show. Also, it was very hot and muggy and in my rain jacket I was sweating like a hippo in a sauna. The walk from Portscatho to Portloe was an absolute cracker. Tough in places with one especially tough Big Dipper at Tregagle's hole but I saw some tremendous raw and rocky coastline around Nare Head. There were still more gorgeous beaches especially at Pendower and Carne. There were also plenty of wow moments and I loved it even though my earlier exertions were taking their toll. Eventually I reached Portloe at just after six o'clock. It's a charming fishing village, has a nice pub and a very close and comfortable bed and breakfast.*

*Just what the doctor ordered. It had been a long day and not without its traumas but it was all happy ever after come the end. About 16 miles I think in just over 6 hours. I'm knackered and about three stone lighter.*

This was quite a day. It started off almost disastrously but ultimately finished on a high. I just could not believe the ferries were cancelled. Earlier this week when the weather was abysmal with gale force winds, I could have easily have accepted the situation but it just wasn't like that today. I really was in a state of shock for a good few minutes. Of all the places where I thought I might have problems with ferries, this was the last one. When you know you're relying on one man and his boat for some river crossings, the potential for cancellations is huge, but not when you're dealing with a large company who operate this ferry service all year round. The inflexibility of my schedule meant I just couldn't miss a day's walking. It would have been easy enough to get to Portscatho or even Portloe by bus but it would mean missing out a chunk of coast path with little or no chance to get back to catch up. Thanks to the lady at the visitor information centre who was prepared to help before she had even opened up and the bus driver I didn't have to. It meant a longer walk and a late finish but I stayed on track and had not skipped any of the coast path. I have to admit that the further I went and the nearer I got to the finish this got to be a little obsessional. The path and my determination to walk every possible inch of it had got me in its grip.

*I walked the SWCP to Portloe*
*All the ferries were cancelled so I got the bus to Truro*
*It meant a very long day*
*But the walk was superb I have to say*
*Off to Mevagissey tomorrow I go*

ACCOMODATION - PORTLOE - CARRADALE B&B Another tidy, clean and comfortable B&B, close to a smart pub.

Day 31

June 9th 2017

Portloe to Mevagissey – 12.3mi [19.8km]

*Went to bed last night feeling a little blue but woke up to a real red letter day. A little peach of a walk this one helped by a mainly sunny day which only accentuated the beauty of this stretch. Not easy in places but more than made up for by its magnificence. It was worth every deep gasp of breath and every bead of sweat. Straight away there is a sharp climb leaving Portloe but you look back at it to see it glistening in the morning sunshine. This was to happen a lot today. You climb steeply to the top of the cliffs around Tregenna and walk close to the edge with panoramic views out to sea and rocky coves and amazing coastline below you. Today's walk hugged the coastline nearly all the way. This eventually leads you to the first "ooh" of the day at the beach at West Portholland. I reckon it's smaller, but marginally prettier brother at East Portholland deserves a slightly bigger one. There were to be a lot of "oohs" and "ahs" and "wows" and also cows oddly enough today. Up again and on across a field to Porthluney Cove and you would have to be a looney not to be impressed by this place. It's even got its own castle behind it called Caerhayes Castle and very splendid it is. Walk away from there and go up a biggish hill, look back and another "ooh" is hard to resist. Then on to an area called Lambsowden where Shetland ponies graze and I did see a couple. At least I think I did although they could have been Dartmoor or Exmoor or Shanks's ponies. As you can gather I'm not exactly an authority on ponies. I'm much better with horses as I used to go to the races a lot, although I often got them confused with donkeys. After passing through Lambsowden the path will then take you down to Hemmick Beach. After that and you do have to get the old walking legs going as it's a long steady climb to Dodman Point all the way to a memorial cross right on the edge looking out to sea. The path today was very clear and well kept. This was in contrast to yesterday's which in places was a bit like fighting your way through a jungle. Then you have a nice flat walk above the idyllic sands of Bow or Vault Beach. Now, if you're thinking come on John, which one is it, then just let me tell you that both the SWCPA guide book and Adventure Series A-Z can't make their minds up and describe it as such. I don't just throw this stuff together you know. I do try to keep it factually correct. You then turn a corner at the end of the cliffs and this really is a wow moment when Gorran Haven comes into view. They missed out another "e" in Haven when they named this beauty looking all heavenly and angelic in a little corner. It only got better the nearer you went. When I got there I did stop for a cuppa and sandwich at the Coast Path Cafe. They serve up very wholesome food and are friendly people. A little walk to pass the beach, around a field and soon up back above the cliffs and around to Chapel Point. Across another field and the path takes you down into Portmellon and another cracking looking little place. Just further on up and around and Mevagissey harbour is looking back at you and of course she is a real good looker as is all of the rest of this classic Cornish fishing village. It was a tremendous walk with never a dull moment. I was a very happy, camera snappy, chappy all day.*

After yesterday's traumas and exertions I was hoping for a better day and I got a much better day. This was a really exceptionally beautiful stretch of the SWCP with lots to see and swoon over. Gorran Haven was particularly lovely [see picture below]. It was quite strenuous in places, especially in the early stages but with clear views out to sea, there was always something to distract you from your exertions. Mevagissey is everything you expect from a Cornish fishing port. It has narrow streets and getting in and out involves going up and down steep valley sides. Looking across the twin harbour you can see where you're going to be walking the next day. It has lots of cafés, bars and restaurants in and around the harbour to be enjoyed. There's also a museum and aquarium but don't expect too much. It's not a Sea Life centre but it is free.

*I walked the SWCP to Mevagissey*
*I liked it so much I was all in a tizzy*
*It was a walk full of wonderful delights*
*With a constant stream of eye catching sights*
*When I'd finished I had to lie down as I was feeling quite dizzy*

ACCOMODATION – MEVAGISSEY - HONEYCOMBE HOUSE B&B It is very central and on the path. I had a small but perfectly equipped room. You eat breakfast in the conservatory with terrific views over the harbour.

Day 32

June $10^{TH}$ 2017

Mevagissey to Par – 10.5mi [17.1km]

*As a keen sports fan I obviously associate the word par mainly with golf and not so obviously with a town in Cornwall. Coincidentally, a large part of the latter stages of today's walk involved walking along the edge of a golf course. Today though was unfortunately really a case of "after the Lord Mayors show" compared to yesterday's belter of a walk. This wasn't helped by the weather which started grey and damp and drizzly and just got progressively worse. Not a day for playing golf or many other sports for that matter except maybe mud wrestling. It was also very tough especially in the early stages with a couple of real calf stretchers up some of those horrible giant wooden staircases. Straight out from the harbour at Megavissey as I've involuntary renamed it with my constant mispronunciation, you're on the up. This is when I always wished I hadn't had the extra slice of toast for breakfast but for some reason I can never resist it. Up to a playing field and walk straight onto some high cliff paths. Along more fields and descend to Porthgiskey Cove and around Pentewan Sands Holiday Park. Just further on is the little village of Pentewan which has a few shops and a pub there but not much else of interest. The first big up and downer comes at Polrudden Cove and is quite testing so early on in the day. This is probably the best part of the walk now from here to Black Head with great views looking down on some stunning coastline. You then come to a very random, large and strange memorial stone right on the path. It just seemed a very odd place to me to have it. I couldn't quite read the name of the person it was dedicated to but I'm sure someone will know. You can either turn back on yourself at this point to continue the coast path along the path or do what I did. I completely missed that turning and carried on going straight ahead. It was only when I saw the sea on both sides of me I realised I'd gone badly awry somewhere along the way. It was a little disconcerting. I had in fact followed an optional diversion out to the tip of Black Head which did provide the best views of the day. Double back on yourself and you pick up the turning by the memorial stone. You then follow the cliff path which takes you into some woods and around a very slippery rocky path. Through the woods and back out onto some fields and the next big steep and deep, this was very tough and painful. It was one of those that when you first see it, just stops you in your tracks and you think "what the hell???" You basically then descend into Porthpean which has a cracking big lovely sandy beach. Astonishingly, given the conditions there were two guys, not in wet suits, out swimming. The weather by now was really lousy. On then via a cliff-top path to Charlestown which is very charming and even more famous now thanks to its Poldark connections. No sign today though of the charming Mr Adrian Turnip who of course plays Russ. A brief stop there and a little look around the historic harbour and back up a hill. The walk after here really is quite non-descript. It takes you to Carlyon Bay and after there to Par via a golf course, a very long alley and quite a lot of road walking. By this time it was tipping down and I was very wet but I guess that's par for the SWCP course. I think the main issue I had with today's walk was that there were very few and limited opportunities to see very much. You were always quite close to the coastline but frustratingly could see so little of it. There always seemed to be trees or woods or bushes obstructing the view. But hey ho, tomorrow's another day and a different path and I'm already looking forward to it now I've dried out.*

I really didn't enjoy today especially the afternoon. The morning was testing but with compensatory views which is fine with me. But as the weather deteriorated so did the walk particularly after leaving Charlestown. The miles between there and Par I just walked with hood up, head down following a route down the side of a golf course which seemed to go on a long way. When you reach the beach at Spit Point you turn inland and walk along a narrow lane past the old china clay works and emerge on a road by a railway line. I then had another walk up a hill to find my Air B&B in a village called Tywardreath. When I finally got there I was thoroughly peed off. My mood didn't improve a lot from there. My accommodation had been described as "a rustic cosy chalet near the coast and Eden". Well, it was at the back of a garden but if that's Eden it's vastly overrated. As for chalet - let's call that a shed and it definitely wasn't cosy. If rustic means draughty and overrun with ants than that is accurate. It really wasn't what I needed after a rough day and was wet, cold and muddy. As always in these situations you've got to think positive and just remember it's only for one night. My main concern was getting my clothing clean and dry. The host was very helpful and happy to let me use her washing machine and lend me a drying rail. There was a convector heater in the room and I used that to dry my stuff out. I didn't sleep well though, not helped by constantly finding ants in my pants coming out of the knackered old sofa bed. In the words of Jim Royle"Rustic my arse"!

*I walked the SWCP to Par*
*At times I wish I'd driven there by car*
*The walk was hard and I had to sweat and strain*
*The weather got worse and down came the rain*
*I think I'll go down the pub and drown my sorrows with a jar*

ACCOMODATION – TYWARDREATH - AIR B&B As you can see from above I wasn't impressed. Maybe on another day it wouldn't have seemed quite as bad. It was cheap though and the lady host was very helpful. It is in a nice village with a great little shop in the High Street.

Day 33

June 11TH 2017

Par to Polperro via Fowey – 14.1mi [22.6km]

We had a falling out yesterday, me and the Coast Path. She was acting ugly, hiding herself away and didn't treat me very well. Because of that I said some unkind things. Today though was much different after we kissed and made up. This love and occasional hate relationship was very much back on. Today was definitely my kind of path walking day. It was a mostly good pathway although wet, muddy and slippery in the early stages. There was little in the way of stones and rocks and boulders to have to climb over. Also, it had absolutely sublime views out to sea with some amazing coastline to view and great beaches to marvel at. There was nothing blocking the view and no elongated walks through fields or woods. It was almost permanent open cliff walking with green pastures on one side and a beautiful blue sea on the other. No easy stroll in the sun though with a few mammoth staircases to clamber up especially towards the end. Leaving Par this morning was no real hardship. I'll just pass on Par and that's probably the best thing for it. I met a few people today on and about the path, this started with a couple out jogging who almost had a domestic arguing about some directions I had asked for. I walked out of Par quickly and on through little Polkerris which takes you to the very striking Daymark on Gribbin Head. You then have a genuine wow moment with a wonderful view and walk down to Polridmouth Cove. Proceed around the back of this very scenic beach, back on to the cliff tops and quite soon first Polruan and then Fowey come into sight further upriver. The sun was shining bright now and they both looked an absolute picture. This only got better the nearer you got, especially with the backdrop of all the sailing boats cruising around between the two. A very short detour to St Catherine's Castle enhances the view and takes you into Fowey via Readymoney Cove. I had a quick look around and some lunch before finding the ferry point. A quick ferry ride across to Polruan and at two quid a trip much better value than some of the much shorter ferry rides I've taken recently. When I got to the top of Polruan to pick up the continuation of the path I had a very enjoyable encounter. This was with two lovely ladies also walking to Polperro. One called Maggie who was walking the whole path for charity. The other was called Caroline who is a Facebook group member and was walking this section with her. We had a quick chat, took some pics and walked a little together. I bumped into them again later in Polperro. It was also threatening to rain at this point but apart from some brief showers it gratefully remained dry. The walk was now getting better and better but also higher and harder. Lantic Bay was mightily impressive and you walk around all of it getting an amazing panoramic view. It was near here that I had the strangest encounter of the day. An older chap walking just in front of me on his own was very loudly shouting, effing and jeffing, slamming gates and generally behaving very oddly. I admit to slowly approaching him from behind with a little trepidation. Then as soon as he saw me coming he just stepped aside and said very politely "nice day for it". Bizarre. After passing Lantic Bay you walk around Pencarrow Head. There is a lower and an upper path here. I took the higher one but not sure if the bottom one may have been the better option. The walk now although still immensely enjoyable was getting very strenuous with the aforementioned staircases proving to be real leg wobblers. But somehow you just don't seem to mind so much when the walk is this good and the scenery gives you more than ample compensation for your endeavours. You just seem to get that extra burst of energy needed from somewhere. On then to Polperro and down into this iconic chocolate-box fishing village with its extremely attractive harbour. The place had a real buzz about it as there was a music festival of sorts going on and it was very lively. It was a truly pleasurable day's walk. More please!

This was a much needed walk after Saturday to revive my spirits and regain my faith in the joys of walking this path. I had been to this area about two years previously and to both Fowey and Polperro but did very little walking then. I wasn't that keen on Polperro the last time I was here but saw it in a whole different light this afternoon and really enjoyed the music and the vibe about the place. I had another long walk, up another steep hill again to get to my Air B&B. It was a marginal improvement on last nights but not a lot.

*I walked the SWCP to Polperro*
*It was a memorable walk which took about 6 hours or so*
*I stopped in Fowey along the way*
*Lots to see there but didn't have  long to stay*
*There was still over seven miles of strenuous walking to go*

ACCOMODATION – HILLSVIEW - AIR B&B Not one I could recommend.

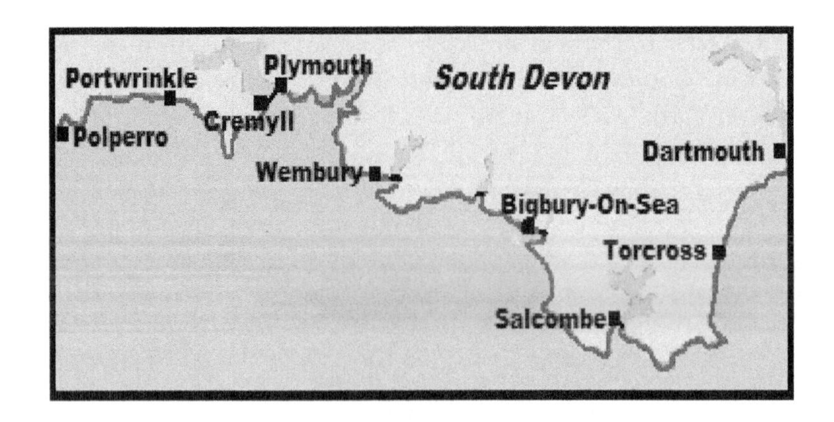


# WEEK SIX

Day 34

June 12th 2017

Polperro to Portwrinkle – 12.6mi [20.2km]

*Had a long trek down a hill this morning to get to Polperro harbour and restart my walk. I much prefer these more popular places early in the day, devoid as they usually are of tourists and traffic. It gives you a much better feel for somewhere. There were just the locals around, going about their day to day business. Anyway, I was off to Portwrinkle today, a very curious name for a place and very hard to write a limerick about as you will see later. A steep climb out of the village takes you up to the cliff tops. Unfortunately due to cliff erosion you have to go inland up a field and then on to a road. I was feeling slightly miffed about this until I caught sight of Talland Bay which absolutely stopped me in my tracks. It was an incredible wow of a view. Lush green fields rolling and curving down to cliffs with shimmering sunshine glistening off the sea. Also, a gentle breeze creating small ripples lopping into the bay. I could have stayed there all morning. I do love a WOW early doors. It sets me up for the rest of the day just like a good breakfast which I didn't get this morning but that's another story. Strangely enough, when I got down to the bay I realised I'd been here before briefly about two years ago, having stayed around this area. It was also here that I first really became aware of the SWCP when noticing the pathways and signage. This is where the seeds of what I'm doing now were first sown. It was like déjà vu all over again".* Walking up the other side of the bay and it was still wowing me. These are the ones that stay in the memory. Back up to the cliffs then and a fairly flat path takes you all the way into Looe. It was very busy around here for a Monday morning with a lot of dog walkers around. You approach Looe from the west side with good views of Looe Island. Once there, you walk inland a little way and then cross the bridge to East Looe which is the busier of the two, with little narrow streets and a beach at the bottom. Before you get to the beach though, the path takes you up a side street which eventually gets you all the way back to the cliff tops. The walk then from here to Seaton is a bit of a mish mash of differing terrains. There's some woods walking, road walking, some low level suburban areas and then around a big field. On the way you go past Plaidy beach and the larger Millendreath beach. You also go past a monkey sanctuary. If I'd had more time I wouldn't have minded hanging around in there. My last encounter with these cheeky chappies was at Longleat Safari Park a few years ago now. They took great delight in ripping all the wiper blades and rubber trim off my car much to my kids' hysterical howling approval. The little blighters! I'm referring there to the monkeys of course! Eventually you reach Seaton and I have to admit I didn't know there was a Cornish version. I don't want to stir up another Cornwall v Devon debate but the one over the bridge gets my vote. From there you carry on to Downderry and you couldn't make up a more Irish sounding name for a village in...Cornwall? You can get here by following the main road or by walking along the sea wall and beach. I took the latter

*route which is a lot flatter. From Downderry you have to prepare yourself for a bit of pain but it's well worth it. A long steep zig zagging, chest pounding path takes you high up to the cliff top. But what superb views up and down the coast you have when you do eventually get there and some breath back. There are still some more hills to negotiate but again all very rewarding. At the top of one of those I came across a small herd of goats blocking my way. I must confess to breaking into a Julie Andrews impression with a quick rendition of:*
*"High on a hill was a lonely goatherd*
*Lay ee odl lay ee odl lay hee hoo*
*Loud was the voice of the lonely goatherd*
*Lay ee odl lay ee odl-oo"*
*Well, as you can imagine, the sound of me yodelling soon got them running for cover. Those are the correct lyrics by the way; thank you google. After that it was on to Portwrinkle. It's a rather strange quiet lonely looking place with not a lot happening. I'm off now to brush up on my "Sound of Music" karaoke repertoire.*

There are a few occasions when adhering to the SWCP associations guide book itinerary when you get to your final destination, you look around, and just think "why here"? Today was definitely one of those. There was nothing particularly wrong with Portwrinkle; it just seemed so small and dull. There didn't appear to be much on the seafront apart from an empty car park and a café which had three customers. I hardly saw another soul in the time I was there. If you look on Trip Advisor for a list of things to do here, you'll find there's a grand total of...two. One of those is Finnygook beach and the other is a golf course. I seem to recall accommodation being a little sparse as well when I was looking for places to stay. It looked a nice residential area but that was about it. I was staying in a pub up the road in Crafthole which was actually very good and thankfully had a restaurant.

*I walked the SWCP to Portwrinkle*
*I stopped in Looe appropriately enough for a tinkle*
*You approach it from the West*
*Then cross over a bridge to the East which is best*
*My final destination appeared to have lost its twinkle*

ACCOMODATION – CRAFTHOLE - FINNYGOOK INN I had a good size double room with a large en-suite bathroom. It also had the largest bath towels I've ever seen; I could have wrapped one around me three times.

Day 35

June 13th 2017

Portwrinkle to Cremyll – 13.1mi [21.0km]

This was sadly my last day of walking in the grand old Duchy of Cornwall but what an absolute crackerjack it was. Let's start with the weather. There was barely a cloud in the sky all day, warm and at times very warm but with a cool zephyr. The path was mainly flat with a few undulations and a bit of zig zagging but no giant steps. It had also dried out now after the weekends downpours. The walk itself was absolutely amazing. It hugged the shoreline nearly all the way, with almost total uninterrupted views of the sea and the coast apart from some woods walking towards the end. It also featured one of the highlights of my entire journey to date, the magnificent Rame Head. I departed a sunny Portwrinkle in the morning with a bit of its sparkle back. Walked along a golf course above the cliffs for a while and then you reach the Tregantle firing ranges. Here is a choice of paths, one through the range if it's open or one around if it's not. Fortunately for me it was open today, because it's a lovely walk through green fields above the sea. It was very quiet, still and serene and I stopped walking for a few minutes just to take all this calm in. That was until I heard a few rifle shots cracking off in the distance. Frightened the crap out of me but kept going with head down. After that is a long walk to Polhawn Cove. Mostly on a path but there is some road walking which I didn't mind because it was all with wonderful views. You then walk around the headland and get your first glimpse of Rame Head in the distance with its mediaeval chapel perched right on the end. It looks pretty impressive at that point but just wait until you get closer. The actual coast path doesn't take you out to the end but you would be absolutely crazy to miss it. It's only a short distance up some steps and the views from up there are mind blowing. Everywhere you look is amazing. Out to sea with a few yachts about or back at the coastline you just walked from or ahead to the one you're about to do. It was definitely one of the most memorable moments of my whole trip. Of course it helped that the weather was so good but I'd go back there any day, any weather. Then follows a flattish walk back from the headland to Penlee Point where you get your first views of Plymouth Sound. Then a short walk through some woods which offered a cool bit of shade from the mid-day sun. You then emerge back into the light and are greeted by the charming twin sister villages of Cawsand and Kingsand. If Cinderella had had sisters like these she definitely would have missed out on her prince. I stopped off for a Cornish pasty and some Cornish vanilla ice cream. As it was my last day I was going to try and make it as Cornish as possible. From Kingsand you ascend to the entrance of the Mount Edgcumbe Country Park. This is a massive estate and the walk is nearly all through woods. I'm not normally that keen on woods walking especially as you only get the occasional glimpse of the sea but today it was cool and very welcome. This is where I had another "animals blocking the way" incident. Yesterday it was goats, today it was ponies. So I used yesterday's tactic of singing to them "There's nothing I can do, if it don't get through, blame it on the pony express". One for the more mature of you out there and definitely showing my age! Anyhow, it worked a treat again and they soon moved over. Keep on through the park and eventually you emerge at the ferry point to Plymouth. I'm not going over until the morning so it was in the Edgcumbe Arms for a quick pint of Proper Job before my bus arrived. A really enjoyable day's walk made all the better by the sunshine and the aforementioned Rame Head. Loved it!

A superb day's walking, one of the best. You wouldn't expect to describe a firing range as peaceful but with the absence of gun fire it was incredibly so, well, until they started then it was bloody noisy. I still marvel at the beauty of Rame Head and the small chapel on the end. The walk from there and up Plymouth Sound is also very splendid as are Cawsand and Kingsand. The last part through Mount Edgcumbe was a nice contrast through a cool shaded wood. In the evening my confidence in Air B&Bs was also restored. After staying in a couple of dodgy ones recently I had a super clean room and the host was very amiable even to the point of letting me use her cooker to make what was almost a nutritious meal. After night after night of pub grub it made a healthy change. The odd thing about her well equipped kitchen was though that she didn't have a microwave. When I queried that, she gave me a very bemused look that suggested microwaves were the latest ultra-modern kitchen appliance that hadn't reached that part of Cornwall yet! This area of Cornwall right on the southern border with Devon is somewhat overlooked. I knew nothing about it but well worth a visit. It's maybe not as glamourous as other parts of the county but very green and attractive.

*I walked the SWCP to Cremyll*
*I didn't have time to dwell*
*It was many miles in the hot sunshine*
*The sights I saw were truly divine*
*I'll have lots of great memories of today to tell*

As it was my last day In Cornwall I included a bonus limerick with a title; Homage to Kernow

*I've walked the SWCP around the Cornish coast*
*I've loved it so much it's hard to say what the most*
*It's beaches and coves, it's bays and tin mines*
*It's hills and heritage, its own language on signs*
*I'm sad from here I will no longer post*

ACCOMODATION - MILBROOK - AIR B&B Really good accommodation in a pretty village and only a ten minute bus ride from the ferry departure point.

Day 36

June 14th 2017

Cremyll via Mount Batten to Wembury – 15.9mi [25.6km]

*It's Delightful, it's Delicious, it's De-lovely, and it's Devon!!! I know this is true as I've been many times and many places in this county, there was a time though during my walk this morning when I was having serious doubts. The day started really well with another fantastically beautiful morning. It was to stay like this all day apart from a short time in the afternoon when a few cirrus clouds drifted over but nothing to "cirrusly" worry about. I left my lovely Air B&B in a cute little village called Milbrook and got the bus and the ferry across the Tamar to Plymouth. There were a few commuters on the boat and I thought what a lovely way to travel to work on a day like this. Too nice really; I reckon more sickies are thrown by people who travel to work by ferry than cars or buses. You would travel over in the sunshine, get off and think, sod work today; I'm not going to waste this weather.*

*But maybe that's just me. Anyway, this walk is split into two halves. It starts with a wander through the rather grand Royal William Yard. There follows a bit of street strolling and then onto the Hoe promenade and forward to the Barbican and Sutton Harbour. So far, so good, I know that not everyone likes this type of walk but his morning it was very enjoyable. There are lots of points of interest along the way as well to enjoy. It was when I got to Sutton Harbour that things started to go downhill. At this point you can choose between another ferry ride over to Mount Batten but this is described as an unofficial short cut in the guide book, so that's naughty and cheating, so not for me. The alternative is the honourable and for the purist, official waterfront walk. BIG mistake! First of all, you couldn't walk over the harbour lock gates so had to waste an extra twenty minutes walking around them. That wasn't so bad but when you re-joined the official path the next three miles or so were just plain awful. You were either walking along very busy roads or trudging around industrial estates and in between warehouses. I hated it and it was depressing even on a sunny day, I'd have been suicidal if it had been raining. It was ugly and even worse than that, totally unnecessary. I understand when there are no alternatives that sometimes you have to do this kind of walking in these areas but when there's a totally acceptable alternative than I just don't get it. It was a little better nearing Mount Batten but nothing worth not getting the ferry for. Thankfully the rest of the days walk was more enjoyable. This started with a walk around to a very popular Batten Bay and onto Jennycliff Bay. Then a cooler walk through some woodland which provided some welcome shade on what was becoming a very hot day. You then emerge from the trees and along a cliff with glorious views out to Plymouth Sound. Next up is Bovisand Bay where all those ferry travellers who had rung in sick where skiving and sunbathing, it was mobbed. Further on then to some quieter parts which was probably due to the extensive areas of rocky bays that were prevalent. A good level path takes you on to Heybrook Bay and eventually Wembury Beach. Keeping you company for this length just offshore is the Great Mew Stone which is a small and now uninhabited island. Apparently, people did use to live on it, they sent the people caught throwing sickies over there. I then had the first cream tea of my time in Devon at Wembury. Cream first of course and it was delightful, delicious and de-lovely! It was a good start and end to the day but like a polo mint, there was nothing in the middle.*

This was a frustrating day especially in the late morning. I felt I was just wasting my time with the walk from Plymouth harbour to Mount Batten. I really hope the SWCP Association reconsiders this section because it's bland at best and easily avoidable with the option of the ferry crossing which operates all year. The afternoon's walk was a vast improvement although more interesting than spectacular. This leads you to Wembury which has a small but popular beach and National Trust café. There didn't appear to be much else here but was pleasant enough.

*I walked the SWCP to Wembury*
*On a very hot day I got rather sweaty*
*The walk wasn't great*
*And some parts I really did hate*
*When I'd arrived at my destination I wasn't sorry*

ACCOMODATION – WEMBURY -WEMBURY B&B Friendly host, big clean family house with a great pub for food about 15 mins away.

Day 37

June 15th 2017

Wembury to Bigbury-On-Sea – 13.5mi [21.8km]

*Oh what a lovely day and oh what an even lovelier walk! This walk had everything you could want. There were river crossings by ferry, river crossings by foot, a stupendous rocky coastline, terrific bays and golden beaches. It had wooded walks, long stretches of level pathway and a couple of right humdinging up and downers. Fantastic countryside, almost constant views out to sea and it even had a small island you can walk across a little stretch of sand to. It had the Jewson lot with whistles and bells, the whole kit and caboodle. You've probably got the impression by now I liked this section: you're wrong...I bloody loved it. It started with a really great little walk from Wembury Beach to Warren Point to get a ferry across the Yealm Estuary. That mile and a half itself was a little cracker in the morning sunshine along the cliff tops, then towards the estuary through some woods and a little flotilla of yachts and boats bobbing away. Just before the ferry arrived, on time, I had some company. At this point four other walkers came along, one lady and three gents. They were all a little older than me, very smartly dressed and well-spoken but there was something odd about them I couldn't quite get. But the ferryman did, almost immediately we got in the boat "Do you all own an ear piercing business?" That was it! They were all wearing between one to four stud earrings in each ear. Now I found that very odd especially for people of that generation. It got me guessing all day about whether it was some weird sect they belonged too ,or, if there was any significance as to how many earrings they were wearing on any particular day. I was going to say something to them but they walked away from the ferry in great haste and disappeared up the track never to be seen again. Oh well, I shall probably never know. On then with the walk which takes you through a little wooded area, then out into the open with terrific views across to the opposite side of the estuary and out to sea. You then go around Mouthstone Point and up on top of the cliff face. This is a long stretch of level path with a gorgeous azure sea looking up at you. Things start getting tougher after Stoke Cross as you head up and down some biggish hills on your way to the River Erme for your next river crossing. Now I got there at about two o'clock and the notice board said you can walk across the water about an hour before and after low tide which it showed as being 4.15 pm today. Well, I had a good look at it and some chap had just walked across so I did as well. It took me less than five minutes and it only came up to my knees. Mind you, I am 12 foot tall. It was very soothing, cooling my feet down and soft and sandy underfoot. On now from Wonwell to Bigbury and it does get tougher but boy is it worth it, for girls too. All this is above an open coastline looking awesome in the sunshine, with the sea glistening away to your right. Then you spot Burgh Island in the distance jutting out from what I presumed was Bigbury separated by a thin stretch of sand. It looks amazing from that distance but you can also see a couple of big hills between you and they were very steep. No staircases but looking almost vertical. But get over them you do and getting nearer to Burgh Island you start to see the iconic Art Deco hotel that you've probably heard about. I missed a chance to spend a night there on a corporate event some years ago and have regretted it ever since. You finally arrive at Bigbury via Challaborough which also has a cracking beach. The walk from the River Erme was long and hard but worth every step and drop of sweat. A superb walk.*

This walk was the complete package and I loved every part of it. There was never a dull moment and it had something for everyone and every type of walker. I always got a bit apprehensive when I knew the day was to involve ferry crossings and tide timings but it worked out like clockwork. The ferry was bang on time and wading across the Erme was no problem at all even though I got there a bit early. It's certainly more strenuous in the later stages but very worthwhile. Apart from Burgh Island and the pub on it there's not a lot at Bigbury-On-Sea. I had to eat at the Challaborough Bay holiday park in the onsite pub.

*I walked the SWCP to Bigbury-On-Sea*
*It was a walk that made me very happy*
*The weather was tremendous*
*The views were stupendous*
*How lucky can one man be*

ACCOMODATION – BIGBURY-ON-SEA - SUMMERWINDS B&B
Probably the plushest and cleanest B&B I stayed at during my whole trip.

Day 38

June 16th 2017

Bigbury-On-Sea to Salcombe – 13.7mi [22.1km]

*Well, if yesterday's was a great walk, I think today may even have topped it. I think I found a little bit of heaven on earth along this magnificent stretch. Stayed in probably the best B&B of my trip so far last night, it was real four star hotel quality. It was immaculately clean and tidy, big bedroom and bathroom and very tastefully decorated. Its run by a real cheerful, chirpy cockney couple called Kim and Tony. If they weren't running a bed and breakfast in Bigbury then you could easily see them running the Queen Vic in Walford.*

*When I was leaving this morning Tony kindly offered some friendly local advice which went like this:*
*"Naw son"*
*"Yes Tony?"*
*"I see those walkers when they leave 'ere all walking the parf but don't bovva wasting your Harry Lime (time) because all the parf does is take you back to the Frog and Toad (road)"*
*"Er, ok Tony"*
*"All yer got to do is walk up the Frog and Toad until you get to the top of the Jack and Jill (hill) and then turn left"*
*Yer got that me old china plate(mate)?"*
*"Right Tony"*
*So I leave and do I take the path or the road? Yes, you've guessed it...the path. And where does it lead me? Yes, you're right again...back to the road. I was too embarrassed to look back at the B&B. I just knew Tony would be looking out the window, saying to himself a la Michael Caine in The Italian Job "you're only supposed to follow the bloody road!" On I went and only got slightly lost looking for the ferry point to cross the River Avon. Just before the ferry arrived and just like yesterday the four multi ear studded walkers turned up. I was studying them very closely this time and noticed that they each had a different number of stud earrings on ranging from one to four. Now I still don't know what it means but I swear the chap with four earrings was looking very pleased with himself! Once disembarked from the ferry you follow a nice flattish path which eventually takes you to Hope Cove. All the while along you follow a very attractive coastline with good clear views over the countryside and sea. Hope Cove is a little treasure and I really Hope to Cove there again. It immediately went on the ever expanding "must go back to" list. It's small but with a cute little harbour and beach and thatched cottages. Also, there were a couple of pubs and cafe's which made it the perfect place to stop for a latte and cake in the sunshine. You then take the walk out to Bolt Tail. A truly magnificent headland and if you go all the way to the end you'll get a panoramic view all around Bigbury Bay and the ocean. Before you get to the end though you go down into a*

*slight dip and on your right is the most amazing V-shaped view looking back at the cove and the cliffs. Leaving Bolt Tail you walk a very flat stretch over the top of Bolberry Down and then a steep descent to the terrific Soar Mill Cove with a popular and justly so, small rocky and sandy beach at the bottom. Big climb then back up the other side but then the path flattens out nicely. Then a steep descent takes you down onto Bolt Head. Just around the corner is that little bit of heaven. It's a cliff face path to Stairhole Bay and Stairhole Cove. I couldn't take my eyes off how beautiful this little bay was. A few yachts were just floating around there which just added to the ambience. The colour of the water was something I'm sure I've only seen around the West Indies. You could have used it as scene from any one of the "Pirates of the Caribbean" films and no one would know. Simply Stunning. When I finally stopped staring it was on to Salcombe which looked lovely in the sun when I gazed up the estuary. There's a bit of up and down road walking now but with the bonus of going around the very pretty North and South Sands beaches. You also have the option of using the ferry service between South Sands and Salcombe but this time I did use the frog and toad. If you ever want to forget your woes for a few hours then get down to Devon and walk the 8 miles or so between Hope Cove and Salcombe. Its peacefulness, serenity and beauty will magically transport you to another place and help you escape them for at least a little while.*

What a sensational days walking. I absolutely loved every minute of it. One of those days you just want to go on and on. I was surrounded by beauty and totally intoxicated by it. All day I was walking in the most incredibly pleasurable daydream and didn't want to wake up. Hope Cove, Bolt Tail, Soar Mill Cove, Stairhole Bay and Stairhole Cove, it's quite a list. This is definitely a walk I will come back to and do again and again. In fact, the place I probably liked the least of all was Salcombe itself. Outwardly it is extremely attractive but there was something I didn't like about it. I think I maybe thought it was elitist but I was only there for a few hours so that might be unfair and wrong. It definitely was very expensive though for food, drink and accommodation.

*I walked the SWCP to Salcombe*
*To have missed it would have been dumb*
*It was an amazing walk in the sun and heat*
*With views almost impossible to beat*
*I loved it very much and then some*

ACCOMODATION – SALCOMBE - ROCARNO B&B Perfectly acceptable but the most expensive of all the B&Bs I stayed in. You don't find cheap around these parts.

Day 39

June 17th 2017

Salcombe to Torcross – 12.9mi [20.8km]

*It was another super sunny morning in South Devon at Salcombe. All those EastEnders can keep their West Hams and East Hams because South Hams is the place to be. Although from some of the accents I heard last night I'm not sure there' isn't a lot of cockney or TOWIE geezers here already. My day started on a rather sombre note when I went down for breakfast. I was the only guest in a B&B run by an older couple. For some reason they left me alone to eat breakfast but they also left me alone with a CD playing horrible depressing "musak". This was a dreadful dirge of melancholy mush of instrumentals from the 60s. I absolutely hated it but couldn't bring myself to ask them to turn it off. I'm sure they play this sort of stuff at Dignitas just in case someone's having second thoughts. Anyway, I managed to get out without slashing my wrists and made my way to catch a ferry for the third morning running. Unfortunately, there was no sign today of the ear stud clan. They must have completed whatever ritual they were here for and their walking of course. On with the walk from the ferry and you first pass a very nice beach called Mill Bay and then onto another little beauty at Gara Roc. The path so far is very clear and level as you walk with totally uninterrupted views out to sea, looking absolutely splendid under the sun and the odd yacht and speedboat racing around. There is then a long cliff path walk out to Prawle Point passing Pigs Nose, Ham Stone and Gammon Head. This is a real pork of a walk. By this time it was getting very hot but with thankfully a cool breeze keeping a lid on the heat. If that drops so will I. Rounding Prawle Point you pass the Coastguard lookout station with as you would expect a terrific clear view out to the vast expanse of ocean in front of you. On then towards a small inland length and a rather uncomfortable rocky path that takes you to Lannacombe Beach. After this you climb steeply upwards and out to Start Point along a cliff edge looking down at a very rugged rocky coastline. Around Start Point and you can see Beesands and Torcross in the distance with a great view all the way up the coastline and out to Start Bay. A nice walk in now passing the old lost ruined village of Hallsands. This is a really tragic tale of a village that in the midst of a long and wild storm literally fell into the sea. There are still a few remnants of housing visible from a viewing point which also gives you the facts behind the whole shocking story. Along to little Beesands then and a longish walk up some steps and down into Torcross. Four pints later and you're at last feeling rehydrated. You just can't walk straight anymore, well at least not until tomorrow.*

This was a long undulating walk beneath an unrelenting sun, especially in the afternoon. The pathway from the eastern side of Salcombe was very pretty, passing a few attractive coves and above all the nautical traffic going up and down the harbour. After this is a lot of cliff top walking to Prawle Point and on to Start Point with nothing particular of note but still great views out to sea. There is a lighthouse there which I didn't get to see but wish I had. The Hallsands story was both distressing and fascinating, the viewing platform has lots of information about its history and how it was lost to the sea in 1917. I had a few pints at the Start Bay Inn on Torcross sea front and listened to a very talented young lad playing an electric guitar outside. I would have happily listened to a CD of his at breakfast.

*I walked the SWCP to Torcross*
*The sun was shining, not like emulsion but gloss*
*My face, hands and t-shirt were permanently wet*
*By the end of the walk I was awash with sweat*
*The weather showed today who was the boss*

ACCOMODATION – CHILLINGTON - AIR B&B Sizeable flat in a small village about two miles away.

Day 40

June 18th 2017

Torcross to Dartmouth – 10.2mi [16.4km]

*The sun was streaming through the loft window this morning with another cloudless sky on display. The temperatures were already on the rise. This was going to be another hot and sticky one! The walk out of Torcross is an unusual one. It involves walking along a low shingle ridge known as the Slapton Line. This thin stretch of land separates the sea from the freshwater lake of Slapton Ley. It's a very gentle start to the day and although it got much more testing later on, overall wasn't too demanding. This was to be a walk combining all the essential elements of English village life and an extremely scenic cliff walk. At the end of the shingle ridge is a naturist beach which I obviously walked straight on by. I do hope they were applying lots of sunscreen everywhere today or there will be some very touchy red bits tomorrow. You then have to take a long walk up a zig zagging path through a wood. This takes you to a road and you follow this road through Strete village. There was quite a lot of road walking today and country lane strolling. Thankfully, it was such a nice day and the two villages you passed through were so pretty, that it didn't seem to matter too much. A lot of the coastal scenery was my favourite type. Trees and hedges high up on gorgeous green hills rolling gently down to clifftops that drop onto golden beaches. Love that. Gert lush as they say in Brizzle. Walking through the village the Sunday morning service church bells began to ring out and it was all so quintessentially English that I actually started humming Jerusalem. Staying on a musical note after you've left Strete and walked up and down some hills and passed a very lovely looking Jenny Coles cove you reach Blackpool Sands. I had to use the public toilets here and was completed dumbfounded when I heard the sound of classical music being piped into the convenience. It was actually Classic FM Radio. I just can't believe I will ever have a tinkle again being accompanied by Tchaikovsky's No 1 piano concerto. Blackpool Sands was actually very lovely with a super long beach. After here is a rather long inland walk through Stoke Fleming and some country lanes before you eventually return to cliff tops. Just on from here was where I had the first dip of my trip so far at a magnificent little secluded bay called Compass Cove. I might just add that the sea temperatures haven't yet warmed up like the air ones, so it was blooming freezing but so nice to cool down in. I definitely wouldn't have wanted to be skinny dipping like those naturalists though. Back on then with the walk and after rounding Blackstone Point you get your first views up a very busy River Dart. Carry on then to shaded wooded area and descend down to Dartmouth Castle and eventually into the Harbour area. This section didn't quite have the wow factors of recent days but was certainly different and interesting.*

I just couldn't believe how long this hot dry spell was going on for but wasn't complaining. Walking in the heat has its disadvantages and challenges but I would take them any day, all day, over the alternative. Tonia was walking with me today and I confess to thinking she might struggle but she coped with the hills and the heat admirably. Something I hadn't encountered previously was the low shingle ridge called the Slapton Line. That always sounded to me like something an end of pier bingo caller would shout out when a particular number popped up. You can actually walk all along the shingle beach but that is extremely tiring so the official option is across the road on the landward side. There was an unusual amount of inland walking today through villages and on country roads and lanes. Most of the hard hilly stuff was early on which I always preferred. We did contemplate having a dip at Blackpool Sands but opted for a coffee and cake instead. I'm glad we did because the beach was crowded and we had little in the way of towels and swimming gear. It's a lot easier to change and go swimming in your undies which Tonia did in a deserted cove than on a beach full of people. We arrived at Dartmouth in the early afternoon and what a cracking place it is. There were lots of places to eat and The Dolphin pub in the square had some great live music. We also had the added bonus of an Air B&B right on the harbour front.

*I walked the SWCP to Dartmouth*
*Under a red hot sun at times it was tough*
*I heard classical music being played in a loo*
*Sunday church bells were chiming out too*
*I also had a swim on the way but not in the buff*

ACCOMODATION – DARTMOUTH - EIGHT BELLS AIR B&B Great location, big double bed but in a small room.

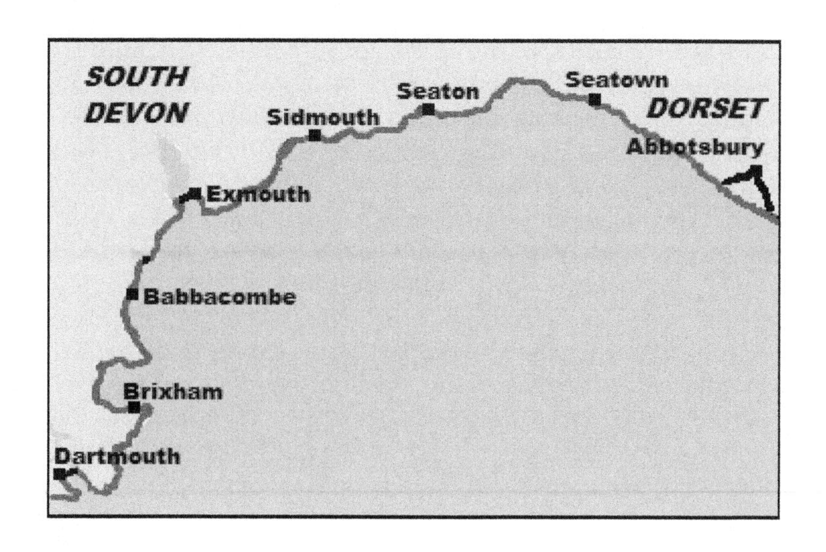


# WEEK SEVEN

Day 41

June 19th 2017

Dartmouth to Brixham – 10.8mi [17.3km]

*It was forecast to be another very hot one in prospect, potentially the hottest so far. Even my sweat was sweating at one point this morning at my B&B in Dartmouth which had a superb location right on the harbour. The only downside on a day like today was having breakfast sitting next to a massive window stretching the whole width of the dining room. It's an amazing view across to Kingswear but it felt like sitting in a greenhouse sauna. So a hot start to the day with the heat just increasing as the day went on. It was a remarkable day in that there wasn't anything particularly remarkable about this section. This isn't to say I didn't enjoy it because I did but there just wasn't a wow moment. In fact the highlight was crossing paths with Kaz (nature girl) Farndon. It was lovely to meet up again with someone from the group. The walk itself starts with a short little ferry hop to Kingswear. Up a couple of hilly streets and then along a lane and down through a wooded area. There were a few of these today which did provide some temporary respite from the rising temperatures. Out of the wooded area and on to Froward Point. The path here is now high and open with terrific clear views out to sea. This walk is quite steep and stiff in places with a couple of very serious hills to overcome. It also offers lots of pretty little coves along the way with the gentle sea looking ever more inviting the hotter it got. One of these was Pudcombe Cove and it was near here I met Kaz. Rounding Scabbacombe Head and the beach at Scabbacombe Sands I nearly got in the water; the climb up the hill coming away from there definitely made my mind up. So, after descending to Man Sands I had my second dip in two days. Thankfully, the water was a little warmer than yesterday. It's one thing screaming like a little girl when you go in the sea when it's an empty cove; it's not so clever on a busy beach. Anyway, with my dignity still just about intact I had a great swim and there is no better way to cool down. From there is the biggest ascent of the day, a ginormous climb that goes on and on before reaching the top of Southdown Cliff. The walk gets a bit easier now and on and around Sharkham Point and Berry Head. There was a real heat haze starting to form now and the glare off the sea was blinding even with sunglasses on and even more so when I broke them. I was getting short of water now but thankfully Brixham wasn't far away. I felt a little underwhelmed when I got there and not really sure why. It was very crowded though and I think by now the sun had got to me.*

This was a hard day's walking made even harder by the weather which incredibly was getting hotter. We were definitely in the midst of a heatwave and it was starting to take its toll. I was struggling towards the end of the walk and it was detracting from the enjoyment. It was great to meet up with Kaz. She is a regular contributor on the group and especially knowledgeable on nature matters of which I'm a numptie. We sat and chatted under the cool of some trees. My swim at Man Sands was immensely refreshing but once I'd dried off, redressed and got to the top of Southdown Cliff, I was soon back in a muck sweat. From there to Brixham I was running on empty and even a nice cold pint down by the harbour did little to revive me. Once again my Air B&B was out of the town and up a hill.

*I walked the SWCP to Brixham*
*Temperatures up to 25 was the weatherman's prediction*
*On the way I met Kaz and we stopped for a chat*
*Under the shade of some trees we sat*
*I also broke my sunglasses and couldn't fix them*

ACCOMODATION – BRIXHAM - AIR B&B Excellent with a well-equipped room and exclusive use of a small kitchen.

Day 42

June 20th 2017

Brixham to Babbacombe – 12.8mi [20.5km]

*"Oh I do like to be beside the seaside",*
*"Oh I do like to be beside the sea",*
*"Oh I do like to stroll along the prom, prom, prom",*
*"Except maybe when, it's 30 degrees warm"*
*That was the forecast for today and I don't know if it reached that dizzy high but it sure felt like it. Phew, what a scorcher as the paper headlines like to print, Scorchio as they would say on the Fast Show or Hotter than July as Stevie Wonder would sing. Take your pick but at times this afternoon I felt like a solitary sausage left slowly sizzling away on a hot summer's evening barbecue. Had a good start to the day when I was*

*reunited with a lovely lady called Lyn, an ex-pat now living in New Zealand. We did some walking together back in May up to The Lizard. I then had a break and she carried on for a while but also went off to do various other things. She's just recently returned from Amsterdam where she learnt all about the red light district on a walking tour! Lyn is a few years older than me so no spring chicken but she is a game old bird. Walking on the level she can shift like shit off a red hot shovel but I would catch her on the hills and as we all know there are a lot of hills on the SWCP to be caught on. We set off from Brixham harbour and in spite of the weather I was expecting a fairly easy day and to finish around 3'clock. I got that very wrong. A nice start to the walk takes you around some pretty coves and into some shaded woodland, then onto a large beach area called Broadsands. From there to a very popular area called Goodrington Sands. Strange place this; it is living very much in the past. They had a steam train running just behind the beach and gas street lighting all around. This soon leads into Paignton with its little pier and longish promenade. Like a lot of seaside towns it's probably seen better days. Leaving Paignton you join the main road into Torquay. It's not the best stretch but acceptable as it is unavoidable. You then have a long walk along Torquay seafront past the harbour and marina and up another road. Slightly confusing signage around here, but we eventually got back on the path that takes you along the cliffs and then down into another long beach called Meadfoot. It was the middle of the afternoon now and hard going which involved another longish walk up a hill before going around Thatcher Point. I was getting desperate for a swim and a pint but we still had a way to go. Also, it's very foolish to drink and swim as you're almost bound to spill some. The walk finishes similar to how it started with a hike through a shaded woodland area and passing some lovely coves and beaches along the way. But the last part of this walk is a real kick in the teeth, especially when you're absolutely cream crackered and gagging for a drink. This is the walk up the steps next to the cliff railway from Oddicome Beach which are extremely long and steep.*

*They didn't put a railway there for nothing. Literally fell into the cafe at the top demanding beer and quickly. They were about to close but took one look at the state of me dripping in sweat and frothing at the mouth and weren't going to argue.*

This was an unexpectedly long day. It was good to have some company again as I was starting to flag a little and walking with Lyn gave me a much needed boost. It was definitely needed today as well because it wasn't the best of walks especially around Torquay. The so called "English Riviera" of Torbay was looking as tired as I was feeling. It appears to have lost its "joie de vivre". I think this was especially true of Paignton. As you move away from Torbay and it gets a little quieter, the scenery does improve and both Babbacombe and Oddicome beaches looked pretty and inviting. Just about there it starts to sink in that to finish the walk you've got to climb up those cliff railway steps and they were a killer! I think the whole walk took about two hours longer than we expected and considerably more effort. I did like Babbacombe, it struck me as though it has retained a lot of its English seaside character and changed little over the years. We were staying in some great accommodation near the theatre. The pub around the corner served the biggest meal portions I had on the entire trip. You got two meals for the price of one during the week for the princely sum of £7. That doesn't mean I had two of them. You would have to have had a serious appetite and a huge waistband to double up on those monsters.

*I walked the SWCP to Babbacombe*
*The hot sun high in the sky did loom*
*Took more water breaks than I normally would*
*So it took much longer than it really should*
*It didn't touch the sides, that first pint of Doom*

ACCOMODATION – BABBACOMBE - COASTGUARD COTTAGES B&B
Very cosy with a super landlady.

Day 43

June 21st 2017

Babbacombe to Exmouth – 14.3mi [23km]

*Noel Coward once wrote and sang a little ditty called "Mad Dogs and Englishmen" with the next line being "go out in the midday sun". You can add "and South West Coast Path walkers" to that list. This thought occurred to me today when I was walking and melting simultaneously along Teignmouth seafront around lunchtime. If it was cooler than yesterday than I didn't notice it and neither did my overactive sweat glands. We were up and out early this morning as there was a long day ahead involving ferries, which ever since Falmouth have always worried me. My walking partner Lyn the ex-pat, (not really sure why she didn't like the name Patricia) was a little concerned after yesterday about how long it might take. We were both hoping for it to be cooler on the expected tough walk to Shaldon for the first ferry crossing. We were right as tough it definitely was, including one absolute beast of a climb. Not too bad in the early part as mainly through another shaded wooded area above the cliffs.*

*There were lots of ups and downs and not much breeze up there. Also the coastal views were few and far between apart from the occasional tantalising glance. This goes on for a while until you get to a great little beach at Maidencombe. Very tempted to have a dip and cool down there but not much time to play with, so abstained. Then it's a real rollercoaster ride up and down hills and around fields and through woods. After the last wooded area you then have that real gut busting walk up a very long hill. It was one of those that although not especially steep just keeps winding on and up and on and up and on further. At least that turned out to be the last one of the day. A little further on from there you go alongside a golf course with a terrific view looking down on Ness Cove at Shalford and across to Teignmouth. It's all downhill now to Shaldon which is small and pretty and the ferry across the estuary to Teignmouth which is bigger and uglier. Teignmouth is a long flat stretch of walking all the way along the prom and past an unimpressive pier. This continues alongside the railway line and beach below the red cliffs which are a now a prominent feature along this stretch. Leaving Teignmouth involves a walk up to and along a main road before going around some fields to descend into Dawlish. This is a very popular little town, with a lot of holiday makers sunbathing on the thin stretch of beach next to railway line. Stopped for some lunch in the square and then back to the front to walk along the sea wall to Dawlish's little brother Dawlish Warren. However, before you actually get there you go over a railway bridge and down a long road which takes you to a cycle path. Another longish walk down the cycle path eventually gets you to Starcross for the final day's ferry to Exmouth. There was a fair amount of urban path and road walking today. It was hard going in the heat but again little alternative so a necessary evil. Just off to find a large fridge to sleep in tonight.*

Lyn was a little anxious after yesterday's long day that we might have a repeat experience today. So after agreeing with Sheila our landlady to have breakfast at eight, she was knocking on my door just after seven to get up even earlier. I wasn't too bothered but I don't think poor Sheila was too impressed as she rushed about sorting out breakfast. As we were walking back to the Cliff Railway to re-join the path, there were a lot of people busy on the Downs setting up stalls as part of the annual Babbacombe Festival. It looked like it would have been a lot of fun. Even though it was much more testing I enjoyed the morning part of this walk to Shaldon much more than the afternoon which was mainly urban and crowded. After you emerge from the wooded valley at Watcombe the path opens out and about the same time turns into a real rollercoaster with one real big dipper. Once you've recovered from that it's a descent nearly all the way into Shaldon with some great views of Teignmouth on the opposite side of the River Teign. There's a nice pub when you get there called The Ness and we stopped for coffee and cake. Once you cross the river the walk takes on a whole different complexion and becomes very flat and long and a little dull. On the plus side it is also right next to the sea so not unpleasant, just not very exciting. The walk to Starcross from Dawlish Warren along a cycle path and then a busy road wasn't so agreeable. The second ferry crossing of the day was longer and much more enjoyable.

*I walked the SWCP to Exmouth*
*It had some big hills and was very tough*
*At times I thought I would melt*
*My feet, god only knows how they smelt*
*When I'd finished my legs also cried "enough"!*

ACCOMODATION-EXMOUTH-AIR B&B Adequate but nothing special and wasn't made very welcome.

Day 44

June 22nd 2017

Exmouth to Sidmouth – 12.7mi [20.4km]

*It was a very welcome cooler and cloudier start to the day, which began with a long walk along the seafront. I like Exmouth with its long prom and sandy beaches. I've been here on busy summer days, you can always find somewhere to park and have a little personal space to yourself to sit and relax in your deckchair. Also, it's the nearest easiest real seasidey place to get to from my home in Portishead. Weston –super-Mare is nearer but I don't count the Bristol Channel as sea. If you've ever been there you'll definitely know what I mean. Exmouth is also the start of the Jurassic coastline with its characteristic red cliffs. Very soon after leaving the front you climb up to the cliff top and continue on to the Devon Cliffs Site at Sandy Bay or Caravan City as it should be renamed. There is just row after row of these little boxes everywhere you look. And what's the most obvious thing to have right next to a massive coastal caravan site? A military firing range of course! I guess that's one way to keep the tourist population down. Once you've dodged the bullets shouting "I'm only passing through" you have a long old climb to the high point of West Down Beacon. Along the way are also a couple of attractive coves to admire low down. Then there is a long walk alongside a golf course and through a hedged area which means disappointingly little in the way of sea views. At the end you emerge above Budleigh Salterton, a very endearing and incredibly well kept town. A straight stroll takes you to the end of the promenade where you reach the River Otter. This then involves a walk inland to reach a bridge to cross over. Unfortunately, there was no sign of Tarka or his better looking brother Parka, the hotter otter. There follows a clear length of walk over hills above the cliffs and onto the very attractive Ladram Bay. Lots of unusual rock formations here caused by cliff erosion over the years.*

*Next comes the biggest climb of the day, a genuine leg wobbly, which is the very long stiff ascent to the aptly named Peak Hill. From the top of here you can see all around some beautiful countryside for miles. If you're a real masochist you can take a walk up to the even higher High Peak but I'm not, so I didn't. At least from here it's all mainly downhill to quaint old Sidmouth, a delightful old style regency town. It's a throwback to the days when these seaside resorts were extremely popular before the masses discovered the Costa Del Sol et al.*

This was quite an easy walking day apart from one notable exception towards the end. The caravan site was huge and not very appealing and neither was the rifle range next door. There's almost as many of these on or near the coast path as there are golf courses and there are plenty of those along the way. I've always liked Budleigh Salterton and once considered moving there until I realised I'm still at least ten years too young. I would think you probably also need to provide your ration book to qualify for residence. The locals really do look after the town which looks pristine. As you leave Budleigh, there's a small nature reserve to walk around as part of the path and if you're interested in birds of the feathered kind you'll enjoy it very much. Ladram Bay also has a caravan park but not on the same industrial scale as the one at Devon Cliffs. Once you've surmounted Peak Hill it's all downhill to Sidmouth.

*I walked the SWCP to Sidmouth*
*The path is now very dry and tough*
*From Exmouth it's the start of the coastline known as Jurassic*
*It was a lovely walk but maybe not a classic*
*And going up Peak Hill took an awful lot of puff*

ACCOMODATION – SIDMOUTH - SIDHOLME HOTEL Very grand but try and get a room in the main building. You might also want to think about dressing for breakfast.

Day 45

June 23rd 2017

Sidmouth to Seaton – 10.6mi [16.7km]

*I spent an evening in a very odd place last night in Sidmouth. It was a grand old building which must have once been owned by a very wealthy local well to do family. It had a wonderful palatial staircase and large rooms including a music room where a choral society was performing. It also had a huge garden and indoor swimming pool. I thought it was a retirement home when I first arrived; the average age of guests/residents was around 95. There were also rooms in an annexe which presumably was where the servants used to live many years ago. I must have looked like one because that was where they put me. However, they do let even the servant's use the pool and I was contemplating a pre breakfast dip. Then I had flashbacks of the film "Cocoon" and thought better of it. Breakfast was great though, served up in a huge dining room by waiters and waitresses in full black and white waiting staff regalia. I felt very out of place and underdressed in shorts and t-shirt. Anyway, today's walk was a little belter. Not very long but did involve surmounting a right couple of whoppers but oh so very worth it. An initial steep climb takes you up Salcombe Hill and across Salcombe Mouth. You then go around a big valley and down and down and down some more to a long beach at Weston Mouth. Walk about ten yards along the beach and you're back up and up and up some more. You're just further along the other side of where you just came from. But we love it don't we. At least when you get to the top of this mother it's a long level stretch all the way along to and steeply down to yet another mouth called Branscombe Mouth. The view from the top is really magnificent. There were a lot of fine Mouths on this section. I felt like a dentist examining all his best patients' teeth one after the other in a mornings appointments. There's a smart little café at Branscombe where for the second time this week*

*I saw Kaz Farndon. This is Kazs local patch and a mighty fine one to have on your doorstep too. She very kindly then acted as our local "guide" from here and so of course we took the official undercliff path to Beer. There is an over cliff alternative but not advisable if you suffer vertigo, the cliffs are up in the clouds. The undercliff walk though is superb with massive white cliffs one side of you and frequent long views up and down the coastline on the other. You also pass by Jack Rattenburys cave quite high up a cliff. He was a smuggler and bit of a rascal by all accounts, probably the original Jack the Lad. Later on in Beer I walked past Rattenbury Court. I wonder if in about 200 years' time we'll still be celebrating the lives of criminals by naming buildings after them, Ronnie Biggs House or Kray Towers perhaps. At the end of the undercliff there is a large staircase waiting for you but at the very top is a fantastic long clear view back up the coast, definitely worth the heart pounding. Downhill now into the pretty little Beer and what else would you drink when you got here but a pint of lager of course. From here to Seaton is another uphill walk, a jaunt along the beach and a stroll along the prom to the centre. I used to come here a lot many years ago when the kids were still a pair of ankle biters so it felt very nostalgic being back. It hadn't really changed much.*

I left the hotel quite early this morning after probably the strangest breakfast experience of my trip. There was nothing wrong with the food, it was great, and in fact the menu was incredibly varied for breakfast. I just felt a little uncomfortable but this trip was all about experiences and that wasn't a bad one, just different. I met Lyn on the seafront on an overcast morning; it was looking like the heatwave had finally abated. The morning was a very pleasurable walk in the cooler conditions up and down green hills and along cliff tops. We had coffee and cake at the café in Branscombe. It was a very welcome surprise to see Kaz again. She joined us for lunch and led the way back to Beer where Lyn bailed out to go to the YHA and I went on to Seaton with Kaz. She's very popular around these parts;

on the walk to Seaton it seemed like every other person we passed wanted to stop and say hello to her.

*I walked the SWCP to Seaton*
*It's a walk to a place I'm very keen on*
*There was a lot of up and down*
*Which caused my heart rate to quicken and face to frown*
*But the views from up high couldn't be beaten*

ACCOMODATION – BEER - YHA Nice building.

Day 46

June 24th 2017

Seaton to Seatown – 14.6mi [23.5km]

*I stayed the night in the YHA in Beer. Nice place but another crap night's sleep in a dorm full of heavy snorers and noisy farters. Had already walked to Seaton yesterday and got the bus back. I was planning on getting the bus to restart at Seaton but as it was Saturday there was no early service, so I had to walk in again. Picked up from where I got to yesterday and then walked along the seafront to the golf club and up along a fairway to a lane. This lane takes you up to Goat Island. No goats to be seen and it wasn't an island so haven't got a clue why it's called that. Then you get to a very strange place which is a National Nature Reserve. This is the Axmouth-Lyme Regis undercliff that takes you all the way to Lyme Regis. If you like walking in dark and humid conditions, with no views of the sea or the sky and on a very twisty and undulating path with little wildlife, you'll love this. I didn't. On the plus side though, I scooted through there in double quick time. A sign tells you it takes between 3 1/2 to 4 hours; I did it in just over 2. Somewhere along the way you also pass from Devon into Dorset. I like Dorset, home to Thomas Hardy and thatched cottages. Dainty, delectable Dorset. When you eventually emerge from this underworld you are soon on to the bustling Cobb which is Lyme Regis's harbour. A nice walk along here past all the cafes and shops takes you to the other end of the esplanade. This is where you have to make a decision about where to walk next. According to the SWCPA guidebook the official route is to follow the sea wall and then go on the beach and walk along until you get to the Charmouth Heritage Centre. However, this should only be attempted at low tide as you can get cut off. The guide also gives you an official diversion and a preferred diversion and if you follow the signage that is presumably where it takes you. I got there when the tide was a long way out. There were a lot of people walking along the stretch of beach in both directions and you can see the Heritage Centre in the not too far distance. So I walked along the beach without any trouble at all and it only took about thirty minutes. You then cross a footbridge and start the very long and steep climb to Golden Cap which is England's highest point on the South Coast. This is the daddy! You can obviously see it in the distance but it's slightly disconcerting that you can't see all of it because the peak is hidden in the clouds. Before you get anywhere near it you have to struggle to the top of Cains Folly and Broom Cliff and they ain't no pushovers. There are thankfully no steep staircases to climb, just a long meandering path gradually taking you higher and higher. However, the closer I got to the top the less I could see of it, a sea mist was now coming in thick and fast. I was starting to think I was going to need radar not a path to find my way over. But the track is good and wide with zig zagging steps and even a rope rail to help on the final push to the top. Once there and you've got your breath back there are apparently spectacular views. Just a shame there weren't any today because of the mist. So a slight anti-climax but it still felt good to have got there. From here you practically fall down a hill to Seatown. Not a lot here apart from a pub and car park and long beach. But it was good to be back at sea level. I knew I should have done some altitude training.*

I said goodbye to Lyn at the YHA as yesterday was our last walk together. She was off to do her own thing and going back to do some walking she had missed out on. It was a sad moment when we parted ways. I had to set off quite early and had to go a slightly different way back to Seaton as the tide had cut off yesterday's walk along the beach. There was a 5k run going on in Seaton and I felt a tiny bit envious as I was missing my running a little. One of the marshals asked me where I was walking to and told me about a very good pub on Seatown beach. I obviously look like someone who enjoys a drink. As I've mentioned previously there is a different feature nearly every day on the coast path and today was no exception. This was the undercliff from Axmouth to Lyme Regis. It is seven miles of dark woodland with barely any sea views and very little sunlight. Nature lovers will no doubt find it fascinating but to me it was just dull and I didn't hang about getting through it. I didn't stop in Lyme either apart to have a cuppa and some cake. I like it but on a Saturday lunchtime it was very crowded. I'm pleased I was able to walk along the beach to Charmouth as the alternative routes tend to be longer and not so interesting. It was a shame that all the effort required to get to the top of Golden Cap wasn't rewarded as well as it might have been. I had got used to being philosophical about these situations so I wasn't too upset. Soon after getting to the bottom of Golden Cap I was in the recommended pub on Seatown beach and enjoying a pint. It's called The Anchor Inn and was packed out.

*I walked the SWCP to Seatown*
*It's nice but a place of little renown*
*I walked from Lyme to Charmouth along the beach*
*Because the tide was well out of reach*
*From the top of Golden Cap it was a long way down*

ACCOMODATION – CHIDEOCK - MERVYN HOUSE B&B Just up the road from Seatown and I had a complete half of the property to myself.

Day 47

June 25th 2017

Seatown to Abbotsbury – 12.0mi[19.2km]

*This was a tale of two walks. It was the best of paths; it was the worst of paths. Ok, that is being a little harsh but it was a real contrast from morning to afternoon. The morning was hilly, scenic and interesting. The afternoon was flat, bland and dull. I had some company on the walk today, this being the two Andy's and Jackie who had previously walked with me from Hayle to St Ives and their daughter Alice. We met at the car park in Seatown at 9 o'clock. Minutes later we were huffing and puffing our way up Ridge Cliff and Doghouse Hill as we slowly climbed to the high point of Thorncombe Beacon. Once there though you have a superb view up and down the coastline albeit still slightly obscured by some early morning mist. Down then to a small beach at Eype before another tough one up West Cliff and down to West Bay. This was a surprisingly bustling little area with a small harbour, shops and cafés. It is very popular judging by the number of people milling around quite early on a Sunday morning. From here it is a short but very sharp steep climb back up to East Cliff with more fine views at the summit. With lots of eye pleasing rolling countryside on your other side this is South Dorset at its finest. Further on along the cliffs and then it's back down to a beach at Burton Freshwater. There follows a rather frustrating grind back inland to reach a small footbridge to cross a narrow stream. A much easier walk then takes you around the back of Burton Beach. This is where the path changes as there are no more cliffs to climb. Instead you are strolling on fields slightly inland of the coastline without being able to see it. This goes on for a while until you eventually get off the inland track and on back on to the beach for the slog into West Bexington. This is about two miles along a shingle beach. It's akin to walking on fresh deep snow. The legs are going up and down but you are barely moving and each step is very energy sapping. You are also below a ridge so no sight of the sea either. Progress is slow and laborious. When you do eventually get to West Bexington you've really earned a rest and a spot of lunch. Not a lot here apart from a car park, small café and another even longer shingle beach. The sun was quite strong and it was turning into a lovely afternoon, but still more shingle to trudge over before the path eventually turns into a road. The walk is better now with lush green fields and views of the beach and sea. It is also very level. You eventually reach a car park and another café which is perfect timing for an ice cream stop.*

*Back then on to the shingle briefly, before a winding track takes you inland and all the way up to Abbotsbury, with it's very pretty thatched cottages and famous swans.*

It was good to have some company again today and it was an enjoyable walk apart from the shingle trudge which we all struggled with. The hard stuff was out of the way in the morning which made for an easier afternoon after West Bexington. Three days later, the path taking you over the cliff at West Bay collapsed, which just goes to show how dangerous walking this coast can be. Lyn read about the cliff fall and sent me an e-mail reminding me of this soon after; she was always admonishing me for getting too close to the edge. After a while I did it just to wind her up. The afternoon walk from West Bexington to Abbotsbury was most pleasant.

*I walked the SWCP to Abbotsbury*
*The first part of the walk was very merry*
*There were big hills and lots of great views*
*Unfortunately the second part was not such good news*
*But I've never been anywhere before that had a Swannery*

ACCOMODATION – ABBOTTSBURY - PEACHES B&B A truly lovely little B&B in the high street.

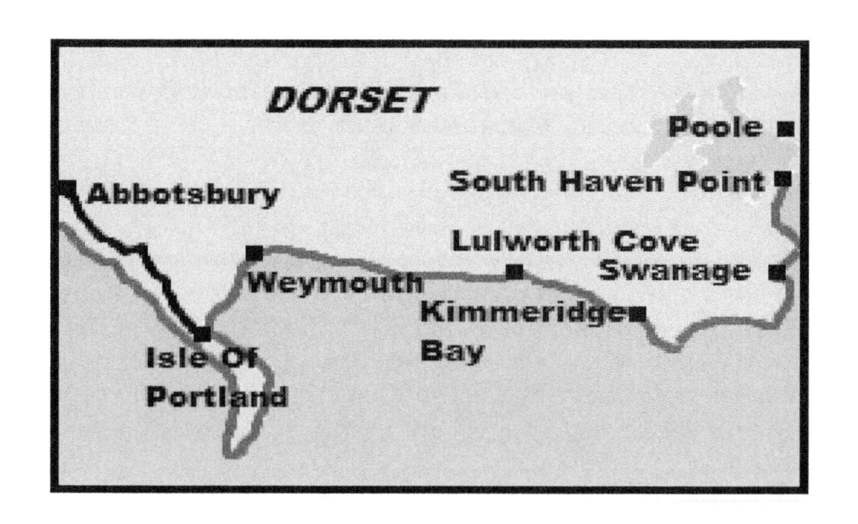


# WEEK EIGHT

Day 48

June 26th 2017

Abbotsbury to Weymouth via The Isle of Portland – 26mi [41.8km]-my estimate

*The very long days walk!*
*When I was planning this adventure this week presented a few problems due to the scarcity and the extortionate cost of accommodation, especially around Lulworth. Therefore, after looking at the SWCPA guide book suggested itinerary I decided to put two day's walks together. The grading's and timings meant that it was a big challenge but possible. However, as we know things that look good on paper don't always work out in practice; the England football team being a prime example. So yesterday evening I was having some misgivings about that decision made weeks ago but hey ho it was done so I just had to get on with it. An early start was*

*essential though and my lovely landlady happily agreed to make my breakfast for 7 o'clock. So having wolfed down a very nice full English breakfast I was on my way at 7.45. I think by about 7.55 I was lost. There are a lot of lanes and footpaths in Abbotsbury and somewhere after the Swannery I took a wrong "un". No one around to ask and swans are very pretty but no good with directions. Managed to get back on track but wasted some time and did extra unwanted needless distance. Never mind, I was down on the banks of the Fleet now and it was a flat path from here and I took off. Not a lot to distract me, green fields on one side, the Fleet on the other and Chesil beach just beyond the water. It's an unchanging landscape for a long way. From that point of view Chesil beach was as much an anti-climax as the book and the story within the book. The path is good most of the way apart from in a couple of places where it's very overgrown which isn't so good when you're in shorts. Anyway, I got to Ferry Bridge in about 3 1/2 hours which I was pleased with, especially as it was starting to get very warm by now. Had a quick pit stop and then over the causeway along the cycle path to Portland. Never been here before and didn't know what to expect. Wasn't the most auspicious of starts when confronted with a lot of new housing and buildings on the far side of the road. On the near side though, the houses were older and more traditional. Very soon after getting to the mainland the path takes you off road and up onto the promenade at Chiswell. All of a sudden everything looks that much better. It has a long beach with good views back to Chesil beach and high cliffs in front of you. Up to the top of cliffs you go following a rather steep path and steps. There follows a long but attractive walk out to Portland Bill. Some of it involves walking through some old disused quarries due to cliff falls but I didn't mind. Once through the quarries it's a nice flat walk over a wide grassy field. Took another brief break here to take a look around and have something to eat. There are far reaching views out to sea on what had become a very clear day. You then start the long walk back to Ferry Bridge along the other side of the Isle, it takes longer as it's meandering and quite varied. This involves walking through more quarries, a short road walk, a couple of very steep climbs up steps on a stony path, a walk along an old railway line and then around the outside of two penal institutions. It's not always right next to the coast but definitely fascinating. Eventually, you finish off with a long descent down a steep path, a walk along another cycle path and return back to where you started at Ferry Bridge. From here though, I had to get to my B&B which was actually on the coast path on the Esplanade in Weymouth. I have to confess this was a complete fluke of planning; most of my accommodation is usually a long way off the path. The walk to the B&B was again interesting and varied especially the part around the harbour. Once I put my feet up I looked at today's mileage. Abbotsbury to Ferry Bridge is 10.8 miles but I think I can round that up to 11 with me misplacing myself. Ferry Bridge and back around Portland is 13.2 and Ferry Bridge to Weymouth esplanade is another 2 miles. That all adds up to a magical number of 26.2 miles. I'd walked a marathon! I've run nine of them but now for the first time I'd walked one. I was pretty chuffed with that, so chuffed in fact that I'm off now to find a nightclub, my legs won't stop dancing.*

This was without doubt the single longest walking day of my entire adventure and probably my whole life. It was also one of the most satisfying as I set myself a big challenge and felt very pleased about succeeding. It wasn't the hardest as despite the distance there were only a few hills on Portland to climb. The good weather also helped as did a good night's sleep. I stayed at one of the most delightful B&Bs with truly accommodating hosts. The difficult part was getting out of Abbotsbury but after that it was quite straightforward. Portland surprised me as I wasn't expecting a lot but the variety of landscape in such a small area made for a really fascinating afternoon's walk. Limestone quarries, a lighthouse, a castle, prisons and an Olympic sailing venue to name just a few of the features here. It also had beaches and superb views from all over the Isle.

*I walked the SWCP to Weymouth*
*It was a long way and took a lot of puff*
*I had to walk around an Isle*
*That took quite a long while*
*My legs now feel like they're made of fluff*

ACCOMODATION - WEYMOUTH - WEYMOUTH SANDS B&B Real old school seaside B&B, right on the seafront with a lovely view of the beach.

Day 49

June 27th 2017

Weymouth to Lulworth Cove – 12.1mi [19.4km]

*Well after yesterday's full marathon, today's walk was closer to a half. My legs were a little bit stiff first thing but a long flat stroll along the extended prom at Weymouth soon got them loosened up. I like Weymouth as it seems to have retained its English seaside town charm whilst still attracting and catering for loads of tourists each year. It also looks after itself aesthetically in a way that most seaside towns don't. Once you've finished the prom the walk gets more interesting and harder. It takes you up to Redcliff Point which starts to give you some great coastal views looking back to Weymouth and over to Portland. The cliffs are now all white along this stretch and despite the gloomy weather outlook they still gleamed. It started raining around this point and didn't really stop all day although not always heavy. The path winds its way up and down and along the cliffs and through woods. It also goes inland at various stages passing through Osmington Mills and Ringstead. Once you've passed a place called White Nothe, this walk really takes off. It becomes a real rollercoaster now for the next few miles with a couple of real big hitters that leave you gasping for air. But what really take your breath away are the absolutely magnificent views you've got all the way to Lulworth. You know every gasp and step is taking you nearer and nearer to those two gemstones in the SWCP crown at Durdle Door and Lulworth Cove. They weren't shining quite so brightly due to the overcast sky but still lit up the coastline and beguiled you as they got closer. I have been here before and seen them on better days but never from the vantage point that I enjoyed today. The path was very slippery now and the steepness of the descents didn't help. There are no staircases on this section so you really need good underfoot conditions or it's quite tricky. I did slip at one stage and put my hand out only to realise just in time it was barbed wire I was going to grab. When I got to Durdle Door I had quite forgotten what a superb beach there is on the other side called The Man "O" War. On then to the very pretty and iconic Lulworth Cove with a few fishing boats bobbing about and people swimming despite the inclement weather. There were a lot of visitors around and that's not surprising, this place never fails to impress.*

I was looking forward to today as the destination is one of my favourite places on the South Coast. Although I've driven there previously I'd only ever walked the short distance from Lulworth Cove to Durdle Door and back. This was a lot further and testing but I was anticipating a memorable walk. Due to the weather which deteriorated as the day went on it wasn't quite as good as I hoped for but still quite superb. I was slipping and sliding on those cliffs a lot which made it harder to enjoy the views as I was concentrating on my footing so much. It wasn't a very long walk so I arrived in the early afternoon and had to hang around a very damp Lulworth until the YHA opened at 5 o'clock. Thankfully, there is a visitor centre where I bought a map and a couple of pubs and a few cafés. I was very wet by the time I got to my accommodation. When I got there I was a little early but someone kindly let me in. I got talking to a retired man and three ladies he was on "holiday" with. It was one of those occasions where you regret starting the conversation because this chap just wouldn't shut up. Even when I was checking in with the receptionist he just kept butting in telling me and her all about his lifelong experiences staying in YHA's all over England. He had a northern accent similar to Alan Bennett and it very soon starts to grate on you especially as you could never stop hearing it. He was aged about seventy and about five foot tall dressed like a Boy Scout leader with ridiculously short shorts, long socks and big silly glasses. He reminded me of Ronnie Corbett. I was dreading he would be in the same dormitory as me but he wasn't. I couldn't avoid him and his "ladies" later in the evening though when eating my evening meal. He was very interested in my map which I had opened in the dining room trying to sort out tomorrow's alternative option route which was vexing me. He loudly stated to the whole room he was an expert at map reading and did I want any help. As my map reading skills are akin to my space walking ones I really could have done with some guidance. However, I just couldn't bring myself to let this jumped up little jerk and his huge ego display to all and sundry his supposed expertise, so declined his offer in quite an abrupt manner. He didn't ask again and I got lost. That's karma I guess.

*I walked the SWCP to Lulworth Cove*
*I've been there before but then I drove*
*It's a coastline that you could never design*
*The views from up high were simply divine*
*This section is a real treasure trove*

ACCOMODATION – LULWORTH - YHA Bit tired looking but had everything you need.

Day 50

June 28th 2017

Lulworth Cove to Worth Matravers – 17.0mi [27.4km]-my estimate

*I bought a map yesterday for the first time in my life. A proper map I mean. I've bought those little city maps you can get but this was a real proper job map - Ordnance Survey Explorer for Purbeck and South Dorset. The detail in it is incredible and it's massive, you could wallpaper your toilet with it. So while you're sitting on your bottom you can peruse the whereabouts of places like Spring Bottom and Brimstone Bottom and West Bottom which were all places I passed close to yesterday. The reason I bought the map was because today as the Lulworth Ranges were closed I was going to have to take an alternative option around them. The guide book gives some directions but also strongly advises you to carry this particular map, although that's a lot easier said than done. However, the guide book is my bible and I religiously follow its advice. If it told me to hop backwards down a road with my hands on my head I'd probably have a go. So last night I spread the map out over three tables at the YHA and studied the route, especially those areas that aren't on my existing maps. Well, the OS map cost me £8.99; I reckon I only needed to use about 10 pence worth. Anyway, off I went this morning all briefed and prepared. Today I think was the toughest day of my whole walk. Physically it was very demanding with a lot of road walking, traipsing down muddy bridle paths and over wet fields. This was before I even got to Kimmeridge to re-join the official path. The official grading from there to Worth Matravers is described as severe which means very steep hills. However, the hardest aspect of today was dealing with the negativity going through my head; at times I felt very low and lonely. Things started well enough but knowing you have to walk a long way in the wrong direction just to get back on track, doesn't exactly help with motivating yourself. I had to do this part though because when I finish on Friday I want to justify calling myself a "completer "and I couldn't have done this without walking around the ranges. But there was a real little devil on my shoulder suggesting things like catch a bus, ring for a taxi or hitch a lift. That's not really me though and I wanted to retain my integrity so kept going. The weather had been terrible overnight but was alright to start with. I kept to the main roads but then the book recommends a short cut along a bridle path. This was awful. Overgrown, soaking wet and now a bog, but once you start you've really got to keep going. At the end of it I was soaked, my boots were saturated and covered in mud and my feet were cold and wet. Mentally I dipped. It got worse. I was now back on a narrow road and decided to stay on it to Kimmeridge despite other shortcuts being recommended by the book. I knew it would take longer but would definitely get me there. This was when the weather took a real turn for the worse. The mist descended, the rain came torrentially down and my spirits plummeted even further. I really did question what the hell I was doing. This went on for about another three miles. Then very suddenly and unexpectedly two things happened almost simultaneously that lifted my mood in an instant. First was a road sign showing Kimmeridge 1 1/2 m and underneath it said "to the sea" which cheered me up as it meant I was nearing the coast path. Secondly, a lady cyclist went by me pointing to the sky with a big beaming smile on her face and shouted without even the slightest hint of sarcasm," it's going to brighten up soon"! She was right, it did look brighter and it did get better, at least for a short while anyway. She will never know how much she boosted my morale with just those few words and her cheery face. Eventually, I did get to the village but then foolishly followed a sign saying" Kimmeridge Bay". This meant walking across more fields and yet another soaking. I did take a short break at the Bay but there were no facilities open today. Now I was starting to worry about what state the path was going to be in by the time I got on it. Yesterday's walk had become very tricky with the rain that fell but there'd been an awful lot more since then. Mercifully it had at least stopped raining but was still rather murky. This is another difficult side of walking. I don't mind hard walks when you're rewarded with amazing views that make it all worthwhile but not being able to see much is demoralising. When I set off up the first big climb out of Kimmeridge Bay, my worst fears were confirmed. It was shocking. You had a "Hobsons choice" of walking on wet slippery mud or wet slippery grass. It was like a skating rink and I never learnt to skate. I must have slipped and fallen over three times in the first half mile and was getting thoroughly peed off. In addition to this, the path was very overgrown in places and difficult to follow, it was bordering on dangerous. I really did have severe misgivings about going on but of course you do. Occasionally, the rain would stop, the mist would lift and you got some tantalising glimpses of this amazing coastline, so I did take a few photos. I was still having to concentrate very hard on my footing because I went over a couple of more times. It probably looked like I was mud wrestling my rucksack and losing badly. The last massive climb was a killer, up a huge monster called Houns-tout. Incredibly steep with no steps to help and just trying to get any grip you could in the mud was difficult. There was a fence alongside it but again like yesterday it was barbed wire. It took me an awful long time to get to the top of that one and I was mightily pleased when I did. After that you descend close to Chapmans Pool which probably looks amazing on a clear day as it looked pretty good in the gloom. You are then diverted inland from here due to a landslip but I wasn't disappointed. It was a very demanding walk today and I'm very pleased it's over.*

This was definitely the day I reached my lowest psychological point of the entire walk. I was desperate to finish this coming Friday but I knew I couldn't call myself a " completer" if I had missed out a 7.5 mile stretch of the path. Therefore I ended walking almost twice that distance just to stay "honest". Even then I knew that I was going to have to come back at the earliest opportunity to do the official path between Lulworth Cove and Kimmeridge Bay. Well I didn't have to but if I hadn't I could would have considered myself a true completer. The first available day for this wasn't until Sat 8th July. Therefore, I spent about four hours walking about fourteen miles away from the coast in order to re-join the official one again at Kimmeridge Bay. I also knew there to Worth Matravers was going to be very difficult to negotiate and so it proved. The ascent to the top of Houns-tout was the single most difficult climb I ever had to do. It was also maybe the only time when I wished I had some walking poles to get some purchase on the now saturated muddy surface. I'm indifferent about the use of poles and think it is purely down to individual preference but if I'd been offered some then I'd have grabbed then with both hands. I was grateful for the afternoon being a short walk of just over four miles and about three hours long. Those figures just illustrate how severe those four miles are. The only stroke of luck I had all day was getting lost on my way to the village of Worth Matravers. I was heading for there and then on another two miles to the village of Kingston where I was staying. After leaving the coast path I took a wrong turn near the valley at Hill Bottom Cottages and wound up walking over some fields. I saw a road near a farm and was hoping this would take me into Worth Matravers. Mercifully, after walking some way to reach the village centre it actually turned out to be Kingston and my B&B was just up the road. I did look up and say thank you. It was the worst walk on the worst day in the worst weather.

*I walked the SWCP to Worth Matravers*
*I kept thinking I could get the bus, I don't suppose it matters*
*But on I walked hoping for better*
*The rain got heavier and it just got wetter and wetter*
*It was much worse than just some pitters and patters*

ACCOMODATION – KINGSTON - KINGSTON COUNTRY COURTYARD B&B Great, apart from the Wi-Fi.

Day 51

June 29th 2017

Worth Matravers to Swanage – 9.2mi [14.7km]

*After a torrential downpour yesterday which continued through the night, it was still drizzling this morning. The omens weren't good especially when I read about a land slip near West Bay last night that wiped out the coast path. But with only two days to go; man up and get on with it was my mantra. Got most of my gear dry last night and so with all my partially waterproofs on, I went out to face the day. After about a mile I was having to stop to take it all off again. I was sweating buckets with absolutely no sign of the wet stuff. In fact, I didn't see any for the duration of the walk. Even better, the mist had now lifted and so I had a vastly improved coastline to observe, which I sadly "mist" yesterday. The walk thankfully restarted at Chapmans Pool as I really wanted to see this after the grey glimpses I got yesterday, it didn't disappoint. Very eerie looking and strangely quiet with only a light breeze to ruffle the sea. The path was obviously very wet and greasy but not on the same scale as yesterday's skating rink. I did stumble once though and grazed my hand painfully on a rock. What was on a greater level than yesterday was a hill name after Emmett. I don't know who Emmett was but he must have been a big lad because this is massive! Nearly all steps down and back up and for once I was very grateful for these. It was an absolute lung buster though, so very pleased that after this is a longish flattish path out to, and around St Aldhelm's Head with superb panoramic coastal views. There is a coastguard lookout station here. Not sure why but they always seem to put these where you get the best views. On then to a place called Winspit. You wouldn't want to spit in the wind here as it would be right back in your face. Further on from here on a fairly even path and beyond Seacombe Cliff is a really striking rock face delightfully named Dancing Ledge. It is actually like a big flat dance floor jutting out into the sea. I'm not sure I'd want to be doing my dad dancing there as I reckon after a few bevvies it could easily turn into dad drowning. A long winding walk follows now with little of note until Durlston Head. There is a tarmac path around here with more terrific sea views. You then carry on above Durlston Bay and into leafy Durlston Country Park. A short diversion takes you onto a street briefly before a nice walk down a grassy open space overlooking Swanage Bay. Carry on around Peveril Point and along the foreshore into Swanage. It was a really enjoyable walk so I stopped at a café and had an ice cream. That's when it started to rain!*

After yesterday's deluge it was a much improved situation when I set off this morning. The skies were dark and threatening but never delivered that threat, at least not until I had finished my days walking. The shroud of mist that yesterday covered the coastline had also cleared away and I could see some wonderful vistas and that always cheered me up. Had a few miles to cover before I got back to the coast at Chapmans Pool but no wrong turns today and found it quite easily. Today's walk was actually my penultimate day and only a half day according to the guide book. As I was meeting Tonia later in Swanage and she was going to walk the last leg with me tomorrow, I made it a full day. This allowed me to take my time and enjoy myself which I certainly did. Once the mountain of Emmetts Hill was out of the way it was a lot easier. Around St Aldhelm's Head the seascape was enormous. Dancing Ledge was very striking and unusual and a local point of interest as lot of school children presumably on a day out were there. The area around Durlston Head was a great little walk on a good path. There were a lot of boats out in the bay there including a pirate ship but didn't spot Jack Sparrow or any pirates. It later transpired it was pirate weekend in Swanage and the ship had been hired for the event. The only problem was it was only hired for the Thursday so had gone come the weekend. Whoever arranged that should have been made to walk the plank.

*I walked the SWCP to Swanage*
*The path was well marked with very good signage*
*I nearly stopped for a dance on a ledge*
*But was worried I might fall off the edge*
*I did slip and fall once and used some terrible language*

ACCOMODATION – SWANAGE - BUDDIES B&B Very good, just out of the centre but big rooms.

Day 52

June 30th 2017

Swanage to South Haven Point - 7.6mi [12.2km]

*"And now, the end is near and so I face the final curtain" Hopefully some of you will recognise these words as the first lines of "My Way". It's been sung my many different people over the years including an incredible rendition by sex pistol Sid Vicious. However, most people associate it with Frank Sinatra. I'm a big fan of "Ol Blue Eyes" although I much prefer his swing stuff. But the lyrics to this classic very accurately described the way I was feeling before my final curtain. If you check out the rest of the song the words are quite inspirational. Yes we all walk the same path, but we all do in it different ways at different times and have different experiences so we are all doing it "our way". With me today on this last leg was Tonia, my fiancée. We didn't know what to expect from today's walk as although we have been to Swanage before we knew little about the area, except that we liked it. I am glad to say that on the last day there was one last "wow" moment. The coast path recommences on the very pleasant sea front. The weather was overcast but the forecast promising. Neat clean beaches here and they spread out for quite a long distance all around the bay. Just the one serious climb up some steps comes early on and takes you out to Ballard Point and then onto Handfast Point. This is home to the famous and much photographed "Old Harry Rocks". They're so famous that I'd never heard of them or seen any pictures but that probably says more about me. I was pleased about that though because when you first see them, it is a definite wow and the nearer you get the more wowed you are. I don't know who Old Harry was but he definitely rocked. They're a long stretch of white chalk cliffs, including a stack and stump protruding from the sea. There's also a mini chalk Durdle Door there just for good measure. Quite an amazing sight and even more photographed now as you will see later.*

*We spent a lot of time around this area as did a lot of other people. Once you've finished there, you continue on a good level path towards Studland and another fabulous bay. This is about three miles long and will take you all the way to the finishing (or starting) line at South Haven Point. At low tide this can be walked all the way on the beach but today we had to take a short diversion. This takes you past Fort Henry which is a small area where preparations for the D-Day invasion took place. There is a long bunker where Churchill, Montgomery and Eisenhower observed the proceedings. Once past here you're on the beach with a long pleasant walk around the bay. At the far end of the beach is a naturists section, on what was now a warm and sunny day there were a few about. Obviously it's only right to avert your gaze when in close proximity but extremely difficult if someone stops to strike up a conversation. Some chap wanted to chat about collie dogs as there was one in the sea. It's hard to concentrate and pay attention when you're constantly trying to avoid looking at a gentleman's dangly bits. The rest of the walk was more straightforward as Poole Harbour comes into view and also the ferry point where the SWCP commemorative marker is positioned. A very emotional moment this as a mixture of joy, pride and relief combined to bring a tear to my eye.*
*Thank you South West Coast Path. I'm going to miss you, but I will be back!*

That was it then, "completion day". A bittersweet experience when you feel all pumped up with pride, but also accompanied by the sinking feeling that this will all soon be over. Tonia was walking with me which was fitting as she had been very supportive of me from the start and during the whole time I had been away. It can't have been easy. I don't think she was ever jealous but must have been slightly envious that I had left the whole 9-5 thing behind for at least a short while, I'm sure I would have been. For the first day ever I was walking without my rucksack as we were returning to the same B&B in Swanage. It felt good but a little odd to have such a light load of just a small backpack. The weather was also kind to me on my last day and we walked a lot in sunshine. It was only a short one and I could have dawdled along but for some reason felt compelled to walk at my normal pace. It was also a fairly easy one especially the last few miles along Studland Bay. Old Harry Rocks was truly spectacular and I was very happy that the last walk had something so good to see. As a bit of naughtiness on my last day, when we got to the nudist area of the beach and with no one around I dropped my shorts and walked a few paces butt naked. Tonia took a few pics of my behind and I did put one on the FB site but mixed in with lots of others. A few people did spot it and I think they enjoyed the joke. The only downside of the day was the actual finishing point at South Haven Point. The marker is fine but there's just nothing else there apart from one restaurant which was closed. It's also right on the road where the traffic queues to get on the ferry across to Poole. We also took the ferry across this short distance but there's not a lot on the other side either. There is one café and a very plush hotel where you really don't want to be drinking or dining in your walking gear. It was all slightly disappointing so we got the bus back to Swanage and went for a drink and food there.

*I've walked the SWCP from end to end*
*Up and down hills, through fields, across beaches, around every bend*
*There have been lots of kind people who cheered me on*
*And gave me support and encouragement when things sometimes went wrong*
*My eternal thanks and good wishes to you all I send*

ACCOMODATION-SWANAGE-BUDDIES B&B- See Yesterday

SOUTH
WEST
2016

Day 53

July 8th 2017

Lulworth Cove to Kimmeridge Bay – 7.5mi [12.0km]

*"There'll be blue skies over, the white cliffs of Lulworth"*
*At least that was what I was hoping for when I left Bristol at 6.30 this morning and indeed there was. The above is obviously a spin on an old war time Vera Lynn classic. This seemed quite apt as the reason I was doing this walk today was I couldn't do it ten days ago when it was closed for military war training. I did take an alternative option but it was a miserable walk in terrible conditions and I was always planning on coming back to do the real thing. Not just because I'm a bit of a purist but also because of its reputation for difficulty and magnificence and it was totally justified. This is such a quiet, peaceful and serene part of Dorset that it's always struck me as incongruent, that when it is closed, it becomes a small self-contained war zone. You can actually hear the gunfire for miles around. So here I was on the first available weekend that it's been open. The army don't train on weekends so let's hope we don't have to fight any weekend wars. We'll have to stick to the regular Monday to Friday, 9-5 wars with an hour's ceasefire at 1 o'clock each day for lunch. It's about a two hour drive from Bristol down the M5 and then on some A roads. You then turn off the A352 and quickly descend towards the coast. Soon you see those huge green rolling hills in front of you and the V in the valley where the cove is. You start to get a real tingle of excitement along with a sense of anticipation. The walk starts with a stroll along the shingle beach around to the eastern end of the natural curvature of Lulworth Cove. Because it was early there were only a few people around and it was looking at its brilliant best in the morning sunshine. You climb up a stiff but not too testing path to the top of the cliff edge. As soon as you get to the top you've got a sublime view across to the cliffs the other side and also the coast path which brings you in from Durdle*

*Door. From here you just follow the bright yellow posts. The path was in really good condition, mostly short grass and quite wide. Very soon cute little Mupe Bay is in comes into sight with its small beach and a couple of yachts anchored up. Unfortunately at the same time you see your first "challenge" of the day and it is rather daunting...and very big. There are a lot of steps but not the staircase type. They do help but so would an escalator. It is exhausting but ultimately only serves to magnify your view of the bay. I stopped a few times and I would just say, take your time, take plenty of deep breaths, take a photo, take a sip of water and just in case, take a defibrillator. Once at the top of Black Rock the path levels out until another set of big steps come along to take you down to Arish Mell. But as we know with the coast path what goes down just takes you to another up and although not as steep as the previous climb this one is longer. All the time though you are treated to the most glorious views of these incredible imposing white cliffs and various rock formations, not to mention the panoramic sea views. However, the views inland are somewhat bizarre with lots of pretty fields to look down on but also a random tank here and an occasional armoured vehicle there. Additionally, there are constant reminders that it is an artillery range and not to stray off the path as there may be unexploded bombs just waiting for someone to disturb them. Following this is another steep hill to go down which takes you to Worbarrow Bay which really is special. It's another beautifully curved bay but with different cliff contours and colours and a super long stretch of beach. From here I took the half mile inland detour to Tyneham Village. The abandoned forlorn village that was evacuated in 1943 with the residents never allowed to return. It was fascinating to look at what's left of this small village with a few remains of dwellings, a school, a church and farm. You can also read plaques inside the houses telling you about the occupants at the time it was taken over. The church is still in very good condition and was looking almost celestial with the noon sun shining through the trees onto it. Well worth the small detour. Back then down to the path and another testing climb to Gold*

*Down and over Gad Cliff will eventually take you down to Kimmeridge Bay where I finished my walk. The beach was very busy and the car park almost full, ten days ago when I was here both were completely empty. It was short and sweet, sweaty but superb. I'm so glad I came back to do it.*

This was a great half day's walk and I was definitely pleased to have completed this last piece of the SWCP puzzle. It starts at the iconic Lulworth Cove and continues over the enormous white cliffs and fields on the coast up to the splendid Kimmeridge Bay. In between are a collection of superb bays all looking very inviting and interesting. Above the bays on top of the cliffs and looking inland are views for miles around. It is very green but because of its military connections the landscape is full of tank tyre tracks and pathways. Also, the odd military vehicle just left presumably until the training starts again after the weekend. When you add to this the uniqueness of Tyneham village, it really was a fascinating area and an absorbing walk.

*I walked the SWCP from Lulworth Cove to Kimmeridge Bay*
*It was every bit as tough and impressive as they say*
*Please be sure to have no doubts*
*These are indeed the Dorset Alps*
*I've now completed the path in every official way*

## EPILOGUE

So that was my South West Coast Path story.

The official full distance of the path is 630 miles but my total unofficial mileage would far exceed that. There was an awful lot of diversions, detours, alternative routes, wrong turns, long walks to accommodation, getting misdirected and getting lost in dunes, space, music etc. I don't think Stephen Hawking and Alan Turing locked in a room together for a week could work that one out. According to the guide book anyone completing will also have climbed a total of 115,000 feet which is just short of climbing the height of Mount Everest four times! I walked a total of 53 days with two lots of 26 consecutive days and no rest days. I stayed in 51 different places of accommodation and devoured umpteen English breakfasts. I carried my 10k rucksack for 51 of those days. I had 11 ferry crossings, it should have been 13, but due to cancellations I also had to catch 2 buses.

I wouldn't profess to have done it the hard way. I think that claim belongs to those campers who walk miles every day and pitch up their tents each night in all sorts of weather. I could have made life easier for myself by arranging luggage transfers. I could have spent more money on better and closer accommodation but would I have had all those different experiences? I doubt it. On reflection I think I was also lucky having good people to walk with so often. I planned to do the majority on my own and still believe I would have done so but it would have been that much harder.

If I was to do it again I would do it slightly differently and have some longer and maybe a few shorter days here and there. I would also try and be more flexible so that if I had to I could miss the odd day, especially if bad weather was forecast or ferries were cancelled.

But all things considered I don't regret a minute or an inch of it. It felt like I was waking up on Christmas Day every morning and couldn't wait to unwrap all the wonderful presents that were coming my way. I hope to do other long distance walks as I've developed an appetite for them now. Wherever that might be, I'm sure this will be the one that I will always come back to and maybe do it all again one day.

If this book has provided you with some inspiration to do this fantastic walk than all I would add is, don't hesitate. I came across a lot of people who said they would like to have done it, but it was too late for them now. That's a great shame. You don't have to do it all in one go, maybe a day or a few days at a time. Even if you spread it out over years, you will be so glad you have.

But be careful, it can become extremely addictive!

Good luck and happy walking to you all.

Printed in Great Britain
by Amazon